Clayfeld Holds On

Selected Books by Robert Pack

Clayfeld Holds On

ROBERT PACK

The University of Chicago Press
Chicago and London

ROBERT PACK is the Abernethy Professor of Literature
and Creative Writing Emeritus at Middlebury College and
Distinguished Senior Professor Emeritus of Humanities in the
Honors College of the University of Montana, Missoula. He is
the author of five prose works and nineteen previous books of
poems, most recently *Laughter before Sleep*, also available from
the University of Chicago Press.

The University of Chicago Press, Chicago 60637
The University of Chicago Press, Ltd., London
© 2015 by The University of Chicago
All rights reserved. Published 2015.
Printed in the United States of America

24 23 22 21 20 19 18 17 16 15   1 2 3 4 5

ISBN-13: 978-0-226-30342-0 (paper)
ISBN-13: 978-0-226-30356-7 (e-book)
DOI: 10.7208/chicago/9780226303567.001.0001

The author and the University of Chicago Press gratefully
acknowledge the generous support of the Helene and Richard
Rubin—Pearl Robinson Foundation toward the publication of
this book.

Library of Congress Cataloging-in-Publication Data

Pack, Robert, 1929– author.
    Clayfeld holds on / Robert Pack.
        pages ; cm
    Poems.
    ISBN 978-0-226-30356-7 (ebook) — ISBN 978-0-226-30342-0
        (pbk. : alk. paper)
    I. Title.
    PS3566.A28C536 2015
    811'.6 — dc23   2015010510

♾ This paper meets the requirements of ANSI/NISO
z39.48-1992 (Permanence of Paper).

Contents

Clayfeld Holds On

Bob Pack's Invocation to Clayfeld

By listening to what you say about
ephemerality and love,
I memorize your memories of what
in fact occurred, but also I'm enhanced
by your far-ranging fantasies, which have
a substance of their own and thus
possess the power to affect my life.
　　The pleasure that you take adds to my own
when you evoke the twistings of desire,
a sheep clothed in the body of a wolf,
through innuendoes and equivocations,
not to be evasive, only to be
accurate about uncertainty
of motivation and intent—
as when a photon beam is flashed
through two small slits in an obstructing wall
behind which a reflecting screen displays
what the experimenter sees: the pattern
of a wave or else a particle,
with double meanings like a pun.
Might not that unpredictability
apply to you and me—each one of us
the other's plausible alternative,
although each double thought remains
a rumination of my own?
　　The waterfall you hiked to in your youth
exists without someone's observing it,
but the pale girl who walked with you
through brambles up the mountainside,
who shared your rapture as the spume
composed a rainbow of its own, she might
be a composite of some other girls
you loved—or maybe you invented her
out of a wish, a dream, a reverie.

I need your fantasies so I
can witness my own life as if
it were a story in a gilded book,
replete with sorrows, disappointments,
foolishness, but still a comedy
affirming laughter aged perspective brings
of how lust lights the way to love.

Ah! love, redeeming love, although
at bottom bodily, first sexual,
yet reaching out to humankind—
such love sought always to emerge in you
as if "Be fruitful, multiply!"
was a commandment to conceive
your self-proliferating self anew.

Clayfeld, my doppelgänger, as I'm yours—
quadruple if you count the two of us
as one—go forth with widened eyes
among proliferating bear grass like
a constellation in the spangled woods,
and journey where your heart revives
the need to reinvent yourself.

The waterfall, composed of molecules,
quarks indivisible, is also
an epiphany incarnate
in the airy ambience of words evoking
your own covenant with Nature,
represented as a girl reposing on
a lichen-softened ledge, her forehead gleaming
with the waterfall's transparent spray—
a girl whose name you might remember
and hold dear. Perhaps you can recall
the shimmer of her hair, her heated cheeks,
the leaf-entangled light that glistened
on her shoulders as you kissed her
and, without constraint, she put her arms around
your neck, returning your uncertain kiss.

And so your memory, though improvised,
completes what might have been, and so
the past can be doubly restored

by apprehending my own finite self,
aware of its own finitude, aware
of its compelling need for company.
    Dear Clayfeld, variant of who I am
in this observer-fabricated universe,
watch over me, attend me now,
and let the waterfall appear
unchanging in its changeability,
its little rainbow lifted in its spray,
and cherished simply for its flowing here.

Clayfeld's Encounter by the Sea

Clayfeld had turned thirteen, and he
was wandering along the cliff
that overlooks the sea on a small island
where his parents stayed on their retreats
and where his mother visited alone
after his father died when his heart failed.
He had to walk through swaying grass
near the bare, unprotected bluff
above a hundred feet of winding stairs
that led to the deserted beach below,
with bleak November coming on.
    A girl sat on an outcropping of rock,
dangling her feet and swinging them in circles
in the windy air, watching the sun
descend in orange and gold radiance
over the ocean's rim. Surprised
by his own forwardness, he asked
if she would mind if he sat next to her
to watch the gathering display of clouds.
    She nodded with a hesitating "Yes,"
and in that pause his mind began to whirl.
As he sat down he grabbed her arm so not
to topple from the ledge; a blast of wind
surged up the cliff as if his blood
were rushing to his eyes, but he held on
although his clinging caused her some alarm.
    Ten years elapsed before by chance
he spied her browsing in a library;
he watched as she took down a book and said
she liked the way the author made the case
that humans are what they have always been.
She turned to Clayfeld and she smiled; he thought
he saw approval in her eyes, and that
emboldened him to ask if she
would join him for a drink that night.

Their conversation probed enigmas
of the human will; Clayfeld could sense
she was impressed with him until
he told her of their meeting on the bluff—
that they had talked together watching how
the orange sun sank in the sea and dark clouds
were devoured by the darker dark.
But she could not recall that day, so she
assumed Clayfeld had made the story up,
as if inventing such a far-fetched tale
revealed some dubious intent of his.
Not so. Either he'd been mistaken—she
was not the girl he sat with on that cliff—
or it was just too casual an episode
for her to cherish in her memory.
    So Clayfeld turned their conversation back
to talk about the mystery of how
minds know more than they know they know,
but now she seemed withdrawn, remote.
Why should his tale of meeting on a cliff—
even if he was wrong—astonish her?
Though it is possible that she was not
the girl with whom he shared the rocky ledge,
someone somewhere must still remember how
those blazing waves smoothed to a hush.
    When they next met, he took care to avoid
the subject of their first encounter on
the windy bluff, determined they would talk
about the human need for empathy.
Clayfeld made some suggestive hints,
hoping to stir her memory, like telling her
he still enjoyed collecting shells
whose colors made him think of them
as sunsets one can hold in one's own hand.
And yet his hints eluded her, although
they talked on in the pulsing night,
but when he took her home, some ghostly fear
prevented him from kissing her.
    Clayfeld decided he would take the plane

back to the island where his parents
rented a log cabin in the woods,
where his grim mother grieved as if
grief could postpone her husband's vanishing.
Again Clayfeld would hike through drying grass
out to the precipice where he
and that pale girl observed the sun descend
as if it knew some secret place within
the rocking sea—a cave beneath a reef
whose yellow fish might sleep and dream.
        Clayfeld well knows he sounds irrational,
but isn't knowing that one is irrational
as rational as human beings get?
He sees her sitting on that ledge as if,
unchanged, she actually were there,
her hair streaked out in the salt wind,
watching the sun descend and disappear,
leaving an aftermath of darkening.
        And once again, in the repeated past,
Clayfeld asks if she'd mind if he sat down
to watch with her, and so he did,
and in a floating whisper she replied
that she was glad to have his company.
He wondered should he dare to speak
of their first meeting by the sea? And if
he can't persuade her that for sure a girl
who looks like her watched from that cliff
all those forsaken years ago,
does that mean she can never trust him or
that he is fated to mistrust himself?
        Whether they really met or not—must that
be ascertained beyond uncertainty?
So why can't she accept his version of
their first encounter by the sea, aflame
with fleeting light, as his forlorn attempt
to say what he believes is true?
        He's certain he must take the chance
she'll think that he is worthy of her trust;
he's sure he has no choice except to choose

what to believe, as it is certain that
throughout the universe red-orange suns
are setting everywhere—endings upon
endings, eternally without an end.

Clayfeld Encompasses a Paradox

Clayfeld subscribes to big bang theory,
with its stunning supposition that
both time and space emerged from nothingness—
a concept probably impossible
to fully grasp because "nothing," the word,
its visualized letters and its sound,
negates its meaning and its sense,
just like imagining not being here,
perceiving absence, seeing emptiness.
    As if this weren't bafflement enough,
the Platonist in Clayfeld still assumes
the rules of mathematics must precede
big bang's initiating thrust, and therefore,
universal laws must dwell
within the realm of nothingness—
a contradiction that leaves Clayfeld
stupefied, and he is further
stupefied by knowing he is stupefied.
    But how does such conceptual belief—
belief he barely can contain—apply
to him or how he sees himself, except
that he is thinking it? Does thinking of
creative nothingness, together with
transcendent airy laws of math,
of axioms and ratios, affect
the way he lives his life or how he feels
about his friends, about his family?
    Is nothingness a challenge to be met?
Are matter's fixed relationships—
equivalence of energy and mass,
along with the velocity of light—
models for moral absolutes
that ripen in the rousing mind:
determination not to harm,
to offer help and to endure?

Clayfeld attempts to picture emptiness,
to find an image for what absence is,
for stark and utter loneliness;
the best that he can do is conjure up
a winter field with stubble sticking through
glistening snow and just one shrub
with just one muted solitary leaf
and not a single partner shrub in sight.
    But then, without deliberate intent,
and seemingly uncaused, Clayfeld
imagines that a cardinal alights
upon a silver branch, which quivers
from its miniscule weight as if,
approximating nothingness,
bare desolation needed something
antithetical—the cardinal
in concentrated, shocking red—
to make itself apparent and precise.
    And Clayfeld speculates his life
might be depicted as a splash of red
against the uniformity of snow—
bold red as an eternal principle
of ripening, composed perhaps
of fecund nothingness, perhaps
the feeling of intensifying thought:
the law of love for family and friends.

Clayfeld Beholds a Miracle

It was an ordinary gloomy day:
the children didn't want to go to school;
they pinched each other and, though reprimanded,
neither would apologize.
    Clayfeld's exasperated wife
had scheduled a check-up for that afternoon
but didn't say if it was just routine
or whether she had some particular concern;
Clayfeld assumed she'd tell him in
her own unfathomable time.
    An ordinary day, hardly distinct
in its fated unraveling; they lost
their electricity, the telephone
went silent, and the frenzied birds
fluttered about their feeder in the wind.
    Clayfeld is wise enough to know
that wisdom can't bring happiness,
and happiness, which comes and goes
by chance, just like one's health,
dissolves and vanishes like morning mist.
Yet fishing in a frothing stream
in balmy summertime sometimes can bring
contentment just to watch the arc
a leaping trout makes in the sun. Clayfeld
believes such simple pleasure needs
to be affirmed and must suffice.
    Their evening plans were to attend
a lecture at the university
by a distinguished scholar who'd been praised
for Adam's Rising, *his new book.*
He seemed pompous to Clayfeld's wife,
with his affected accent and bow tie,
though he was born here in the States.
    The microphone, projected forward from
its hinge, adjusted to his height,

was tapped to check the level of its sound,
and he proceeded in his unctuous tones
to flaunt his erudition to the world:
"And God created every living orgasm,"
were the exact words that escaped his lips.

A great collective gasp erupted from
the audience; laughter cascaded out
beyond control, beyond imagining
what anyone attending might have wished.
He tried in vain to recompose himself,
but then a miracle occurred despite
all odds against its likelihood.

The microphone, erect in air, began
slowly to droop—slowly as in a dream;
appalled, the stooping scholar stood transfixed,
since some mischievous divinity
had intervened thus to reveal himself.

If one knows Clayfeld well enough,
one might suspect he made this story up
to prove that on an ordinary day—
a day with no particular regrets—
miraculous laughter can appear,
suffusing the astounded universe.

Clayfeld, of course, has made up jokes before,
although he swears upon his faithful Muse
the miracle described above
occurred precisely as presented here.
What reason other than to conjure laughter that
can bring relief to ordinary life
might Clayfeld have to lie to anyone?

Clayfeld Attends a Seder

Clayfeld accepts an invitation to
break matzoh with his rabbi friend
on Seder night, and yet before they share
the bitter herbs that symbolize
the ancient story of affliction,
Clayfeld relates an incident of what
his young son told him many years ago
after the last Israeli war.
　　Clayfeld informs his friend it was
a family routine that when
their third-grade son came home from school,
they would discuss what he had studied
on that day. Clayfeld believes
a father is obliged to help his child
distinguish those opinions based on facts
from biases to which we all are prone.
　　One day, roused Clayfeld recollects,
his son was just reluctant to converse;
when Clayfeld urged him to describe
something significant he learned at school,
he answered that they'd studied how
the prophet, Moses—even though
a stutterer who did not want to be
the one to challenge Pharaoh's rule—
was ordered by Yahweh Himself
to liberate the Jews from slavery.
　　Clayfeld could tell his son was moved
as he recounted how Pharaoh commanded
that his Hebrew slaves be whipped
and made to work by baking bricks
in the harsh sun, and he was troubled when
God then inflicted ten great plagues,
including clouds of swarming locusts,
multitudes of slimy frogs, and death
to each first-born Egyptian son,

to force this stubborn pharaoh to allow
the long-tormented people to go free
and settle in a country of their own
in what they called The Promised Land.

Clayfeld remembers this as if
it were just yesterday—reliving how
his son went strangely still. But Clayfeld
pressed him to continue talking since
he, too, was puzzled when God hardened
Pharaoh's heart so that he changed his mind
and stopped the freeing of the Jews,
though freeing them for good was what
God wanted Moses to achieve.

Clayfeld enquired how then did all
the fleeing Jews escape across the sea—
how did they manage to survive with just
unleavened bread and bitter herbs—
to seek the land God promised them?

His son gave him a probing look and said—
Clayfeld recalls his very words—
"Don't worry, Dad, you'll like the way
the story ends: Moses instructed
his inventive engineers to build a bridge
across the sea, and when he saw
Egyptian soldiers coming after them,
Moses commanded the Israeli Air Force
to attack and bomb the bridge so that
the soldiers couldn't capture them
and turn them into slaves again.
The whole Egyptian army drowned."

Clayfeld recalls he asked his son
if that's the story of the exodus
the students had been taught at school,
and with the slight hint of a smile,
he looked right into Clayfeld's eyes:
"I don't think, Dad, that you'd believe me if
I told you what our teacher really *said.*"

"I hope, dear friend, you don't think I
invented this amusing memory

merely to entertain your Seder feast,
but to remind you that next year
we'll be united in Jerusalem,
though that may take another miracle."

Clayfeld Admonishes the Bard

Clayfeld reads Shakespeare late into the night
and thinks that if the plays were his,
he'd write them all as comedies.
To lighten fears of some mad terrorist attack,
Clayfeld imagines how he would revise
Hamlet *into a festive play,*
including an exchange of binding vows,
a wedding dance with shapely girls
inside a garden with a fountain
and white marble-sculpted deities
beside a stream with drifting swans.
 Clayfeld would have Hamlet arrive in time
to pull depressed Ophelia from the stream,
and when her senses are restored,
Hamlet in the last act will marry her
according to his mother's devout wish.
 Hamlet will make a full recovery
from wounds inflicted on him in the duel
contrived by lustful Claudius,
and will assume his rightful throne,
forgive contrite Laertes, and then rule
in Denmark into ripe old age.
 And so with just a little tweaking
of the plot, an improvising Clayfeld
thus contrives to satisfy his audience.
What's wrong with that? Clayfeld contends
with his own self. Can't lasting joy be found
in marriages and reconciliations
and reunions, in lush summer scenery?
Can't one embrace an optimistic view
of human motivation even though
rotten old Denmark has begun to stink?
Why not have faith that love and loyalty
are able to survive beyond the rapture
that initially evokes love's vows,

the faith to trust in seeking peace?
And for an instant Clayfeld does succeed,
surrounded by white statues and white swans,
in overcoming his own doubts.

But then his darker self enquires:
what consolation, unrelenting bard,
do you propose in taking arms
against the unrelenting sea
if we're controlled by misalignment
of the whirling stars, mere puppets
of indifferent or malicious gods,
and if disaster lurks within our blood?
Is nothing to be done but share
in your expression of your grief?

Your weeping art, is it no more
than an impassioned plea for us
to hold on and endure, if only for
the simple sake of holding on
in this, our "interim" in Denmark, as
it's always been, as it is now, so that
despite our aching wishes and our hopes,
unchanging as the sea, we live
preparing to outface the worst
before descending silence intervenes:
Fortinbras's soldiers firing in the street?

Clayfeld Defines Sublimity

So melancholy Clayfeld brings to mind
George Bernard Shaw's instructions
that will bring the closing curtain down
in his play, *Man and Superman:*
"Universal laughter"—laughter contrived
to last eternity, thus lovers' talk,
life's fecund overflow, will have no end.
Clayfeld imagines laughter rippling through
the audience up to the balcony,
into the wings, the corridors; laughter
flows out into the street, up to the sky,
and on into the star-lit universe.
    "Sublime!" Clayfeld extemporizes
to himself, as when God says to Sarah,
who is well past menopause,
that she at last will give birth to a child.
She laughs out loud in disbelief,
even as Yahweh seems to take offense
at wrinkled Sarah's doubting Him;
she laughs at the divine absurdity and names
her infant Isaac, meaning he-who-laughs,
her version of a miracle of words
that even Clayfeld can find credible.
    Such is the laughter of sublimity,
Clayfeld reiterates out loud, as when
Hector's small son recoils with fear
at the stiff horsehair crest that waves above
the shining helmet his tall father wears;
he cringes at his nurse's breast as Hector,
knowing how deep human terror lies,
removes his helmet as he stoops to kiss his son;
he laughs together with his laughing wife,
despite the fact he knows a greater terror
still awaits him at his destined end.

It is indeed sublime—this combination
of extremities: torment and joy,
sadness and happiness—so Clayfeld
speculates, as when despondent Troilus,
deserted and betrayed by love,
is speared by rampaging Achilles though
he rises through the planetary spheres
above the earth and looks back at
the little plot of earth, this pulsing O,
surrounded by the undulating sea,
where he can see himself still mourning while
ferocious battle rages as before.
    And yet Clayfeld remembers that
ascended Troilus laughs despite
the multitude of tears he's shed
at what he sees diminished down below:
love's unrequited promises and vows.
    And at the uttermost extremity,
Clayfeld can see storm-ravaged old King Lear,
imprisoned with his daughter, fair Cordelia,
after their vain armies suffer a defeat.
Lear claims that they will overcome blind fate,
the certain rise and fall of empires, thus
outlasting lunar time itself;
they'll laugh at "gilded butterflies,"
the fleeting beauty of all fleeting things,
and for an instant butterflies
well represent what beauty
fragile life is able to contain.
    Lear's laughter is not merely laughter
of the circumstantial here and now,
not merely funny and not meant
to settle scores or even grievances.
His is the laughter of sublimity
incarnate yet strangely detached;
his is the laughter of the humming spheres,
having emerged from mud and slime,
renewing and renewable.

And to embrace such laughter, lilting
lighter than loose airy particles, Clayfeld
once more aspires to reinvent himself.

Clayfeld Goes Birding

Clayfeld enjoys identifying birds
as if it were the complement
of introspection into his own self.
He thinks he knows how Adam felt when God
commanded him to name the animals,
although he has no wish to take
dominion over anyone; in fact,
he often doesn't know what bird alights
to preen its striped wings on a nearby branch.
　　Annunciating Clayfeld is confused,
especially in autumn when he spots,
so he assumes, a yellow warbler
who's obscured among the maple leaves:
maybe it is a Wilson's warbler or
a female hooded warbler. Males—
according to the Peterson guide book—
are recognizable by sleek black heads
illuminated in the glare of noon.
　　In Roger Tory Peterson's
essential book—the watcher's bible,
one might say—there is a section called
"confusing autumn warblers," which provides
personal consolation to vexed Clayfeld,
since he thinks of Peterson as his
companion in uncertainty.
　　Clayfeld is tempted to give up, unless
it is a pileated woodpecker
that's mercifully unmistakable,
though he's encouraged when he can make out
a warbler from a vireo or if
he's able to identify a redstart
with its bold display of orange wings.
　　But Clayfeld rarely knows for sure.
Uncertainty is palpable to him,
as if it had a form that he could see—

a form depicting change itself—
as birds change gaudy plumage through
the seasons cycling in their rounds
and make themselves increasingly
elusive and more difficult to name.

    Clayfeld imagines Peterson might
equally be watching him—a tough old bird
distinguished by his quackery, although
he wonders if he is elusive too.
Would anyone who knew him as a boy,
so muscular and smooth, be able to
identify him now but for the shade
residing in his strained, inquiring eyes?

    Clayfeld assumes he also has become
an expert in uncertainty,
a connoisseur of hunches, speculations,
and surmises postulated on
no more than variations on the wing bars
and the tail configurations of
confusing warblers in soft shifting
autumn light amid the agitated leaves.

    Yet, pausing, Clayfeld is at peace
with such uncertainty; he feels at home
not knowing what he cannot know—
the contradictions that define him now
between acceptance and desire.

    Perhaps the pleasure of identifying
evanescent birds, the flaring colors
in receding light, is there for anyone
who cares enough to pause and see
and cherish as their own; and if
such pleasure in the names one gives
is what connecting empathy allows,
Clayfeld can be content to watch his birds
as evening settles in the laden boughs.

A Blue Heron Appears to Clayfeld
for Dan Spencer

Meandering along the riverbank,
accompanied by his like-minded friend,
Clayfeld observes a blue-gray heron
with its neck curled back, its long thin legs
stretched out behind the whir of wings,
streak right above the roiling river's flow.
But Clayfeld wants to offer more
than wordless awe as his response;
he wishes to participate somehow
in that surprising spectacle,
to pluck from unresponsive silence
a fine shimmering analogy
to share with his uplifted friend.
 Clayfeld wants his enjoyment of
the rhythm of the heron's giant wings,
the river undulating under him,
to amplify what he and his tall friend
had witnessed just a flash ago.
 But nothing comes to mind; the shock of blue
resists comparison as if the bird
must not be seen as more than its own self,
as if Clayfeld's observing him
contributes nothing to the scene—and yet
Clayfeld's perceived irrelevance invites
acknowledgment, which somehow then provides
a misty aura for the spectacle.
 Extemporizing to his friend,
as he is wont to do, Clayfeld would thus
include himself as part of the event,
and he reiterates the whir and streak
of unanticipated white and blue,
the plumed black line above the heron's eye,
the dagger glint of its extended bill.

So Clayfeld's voice ascends above
his normal baritone as he declaims
that his awareness of the heron's
separate, unique identity
released in him a surge of pleasure
instantaneous as the blue heron's
passing over undulating water with
its ice floes glowing in the midday sun.
    And Clayfeld's lanky friend lifts up
tip-toe to his exalted height,
flapping his long arms like a heron's wings,
revealing that he might have been
a heron in a prior life, cascading over
this same river in the hurtling wind;
and maybe Clayfeld was a heron too—
why not? They share a common heritage,
his friend proclaims, a common fate.
    A grayish blur of blue, the heron
disappears around the river bend,
and Clayfeld's improvising friend,
his outstretched arms still wavering,
glides down within himself and settles
smoothly on the stony shore
before astonished Clayfeld's gaze; and there,
poised in the winter sun, he shines forth
permanent and palpable in actual
friendship's legendary light
with his imaginary folded wings.

Clayfeld's Kidney
for Richard Rubin

A mild wind murmurs wooingly
among the blossoms of his apple trees,
and Clayfeld wills himself to keep
his senses focused on the feeling that
he momentarily enjoys as if
its repetition in his mind
will help him face whatever aftermath
is yet to follow the cessation of
the scented, lullabying wind.
    Yet maybe the conceiving mind possesses
satisfactions it can call
its own—gratifications capable
of being generated by itself,
affirming value in a concept,
an abstraction such as generosity.
    Clayfeld recalls his boyhood friend
who had one kidney that he feared
might fail and need to be replaced,
so Clayfeld offered one of his
should the necessity arise.
His friend, however, was a left-of-center
liberal, while Clayfeld would insist
our founding Constitution should
be rigidly interpreted.
His friend, who liked to rib him, claimed
that he was apprehensive Clayfeld's
right-of-center kidney might subvert
his own heartfelt political beliefs.
    Clayfeld can't stomach ideology;
it stifles open-ended thought,
denies the body's clumsiness.
Better to speak in awkward metaphors,
evoking the emotions of ideas,

their underlying contradictions
and uncertainties; better
to bite your tongue than falsify
complexities and ambiguities.

    Before a medical decision could be
finalized, a younger donor's kidney
suddenly became available,
and Clayfeld's offer, not without
ambivalent relief, went unfulfilled.

    Yet Clayfeld still took credit for
the gesture he had made without
return advantage to himself—except
the satisfaction of the thought,
plucked from the empyrean of his mind,
of helping someone whom he cared about.

    Hardheaded Clayfeld won't rule out
the possibility his kidney might
have modified, not his friend's politics,
but his awareness of dependency;
it even might have changed the way
his friend was able to regard
how his worn senses had acquired
a new intensity in apprehending
sensual delight—as if
the murmuring of summer wind amid
a grove of apple trees were welcoming
and personal because he'd be preparing
for long winter that comes afterward.

    But Clayfeld interrupts his reverie
about his left-of-center friend,
knowing that thinking of him now
as transformed so that he resembles
Clayfeld's fantasizing self
must constitute its own reward.

    Thus constitutionally altered by
receiving a spare kidney in
a willfully imagined gesture of
presumptive brotherhood, Clayfeld's

rejuvenated friend returns
the offering by buying him a tree
to plant amid his aging apple grove.

Clayfeld Observes a Herd of Elk

A herd of elk—a hundred, maybe more—
all head in one direction up a slope,
across a field, to reach the tangled woods
as Clayfeld spies their white receding rumps
composing the stark panoramic scene.
"Is Nature mooning me?" Clayfeld enquires
out loud, although he does not
take offense. "It's best that one's relationship
with Nature be contemplative,
impersonal," Clayfeld hypothesizes
to the breeze unwinding into forest shade.
      Clayfeld considers what his thoughts
might be if he were now assaulted by
a hungry grizzly bear. "That's how
ongoing Nature works," he ruminates.
"The bear has no hostility toward me;
I fully understand his point of view."
And Clayfeld takes some satisfaction in
this generously broad philosophy.
      The elk veer to the left in unison,
their undulating rumps uplifted
as they leap into a patch of light—as if
to emphasize the message Clayfeld's gift
for fanciful interpretation still
provides him with in order to help him
affirm the laws of Nature as they are.
The image of elks mooning him
makes Clayfeld feel he has a role to play,
that Nature must be pleased to have him
in attendance watching there.
      And yet his fantasy of being mauled
by a big bear presents a complication
Clayfeld reasons needs to be resolved.
He wonders just how much detachment
he'd be able to maintain

while being munched on by a bear.
Maybe he could break free from its huge grip
and spin around, and drop his pants
so he could moon the thwarted bear
who, in astonishment, would surely
back right off so he could get away
to live out his own interval between
preserving laughter and oblivion.

"Ridiculous!" Clayfeld acknowledges
in blushing self-admonishment,
although he is amused by his imagining
because it tweaks his weakness for
rebellious anarchy against the laws
of Nature that confine him to accept
the limitations of his creaturehood.

Clayfeld decides the time has come for him
to show bravado and to demonstrate
defiance of Nature's restrictions that
his agitated spirit has endured,
and moon the whole indifferent universe.

Behold! He contemplates his pristine ass
now orbiting the earth, a double moon
astounding the terrestrial
astronomers—a constellation brighter
even than bright Orion, that adds to Nature
an illumination pulsing in the sky,
asserting a preferred position there.

Clayfeld Organizes His Jokes

    Clayfeld decides he needs to organize
his jokes in categories and by theme
because without his favorites he can't
control his fears, contain his grievances.
    Illusions, like a blissful afterlife,
or like the wish to make society more just
for the downtrodden and the destitute,
are just temptations that he must
relinquish and then cast away.
Clayfeld believes jokes help replace
high-mindedness with ordinary facts,
as when a beggar, chutzpah in his heart,
assumes his suffering deserves
some worldly recompense, and so
he prays to God that he might win
the jackpot lottery. Yet he must be
reminded by an angel in a dream
he's got to buy a ticket first.
Clayfeld can easily identify with him.
    Now in a time of illness and decline,
consoling jokes come flooding back,
making humiliations and defeats
endurable if only in a pause
when triumph over odds seems possible.
So Clayfeld places jokes in groups
to help him cherish and remember them.
    One group conveys ambivalence,
since Clayfeld knows he can admire someone
yet feel competitive up to the edge
of sharp hostility. Wit can relieve
such animosity, anger can be deflected or
contained just as when Bernard Shaw
offered two tickets to the opening
of his new play, *Pygmalion*,
to Winston Churchill, urging him

to bring a friend—if he had one.
Churchill regretfully replied that he
was not free to attend opening night,
but would Shaw kindly send two tickets for
the next performance—if there should be one.

    No longer able to hike up a mountainside
or swim across a lake, Clayfeld knows well
the body is the ultimate reality,
desires trump ideals; we can't escape
demands our senses make on us
or override our fantasies.

    Laughter allows glum Clayfeld to maintain
his grim allegiance to this world and still
find satisfaction in his aching loves.
And thus when Diane Keaton says
to Woody Allen, "Sex without true love
is just a hollow act, a meaningless
experience," Woody replies, "Of all
hollow experiences that I know,
sex is the best." Clayfeld repeats this joke,
and sharing it brings him relief
from wishing to renounce his own desires.

    And Clayfeld knows his words enable him
to take delight in playfulness and mean
what their allusions broaden them to mean,
so that wide-smiling Kermit, puppet frog
extraordinaire, can be inspired to quip
that "time is fun when you are having flies."

    There are worse ways than making puns
to pass time and to free ourselves
from what Clayfeld considers phoniness,
from aspirations to transcend
the limitations Nature lays on us.

    Having achieved much fame and wealth,
the Jewish Groucho Marx receives
an invitation to become a member of
a posh exclusive country club,
but he declines by reasoning that he
has no wish to belong to any club that would

accept the likes of him. Clayfeld admires
audacity confronting privilege.

   Anarchic at their punful hearts,
jokes thumb their noses at restraints and rules,
the logic of the world whose laws oppress;
within our rebel fantasies we triumph
over forces that restrain desire
as if we were like deities designed
for pleasure and for immortality.

   Despite his moment of elation, still
another joke arises now in Clayfeld's mind:
Jacob and Saul are caught by the Gestapo and
they're brought before a firing squad.
The spotless captain offers them a chance
to speak some farewell words.
Jacob requests a cigarette, but Saul
hisses pragmatically in Jacob's ear:
"Shut up for once, don't ask for trouble, you
are only going to piss the bastards off."

   What can conflicted Clayfeld say about
a joke like this? Does it belong
in some weird category by itself?
Can laughter of this kind relieve
the pain caused by our cruelty,
converting sorrow for an instant so
the unacceptable appears acceptable?
What other power might Clayfeld possess
to hold back the unfathomable dark?

Confronting Clayfeld

Pausing for breath on a large fallen tree,
Clayfeld must have been watching longer
than he realized, for now declining light
upon the snow-bedazzled mountaintop
reveals blue shades and purple shadows
down its crevices that guide his view
to where the thrusting tree line ends,
the swaying tips of evergreens.
    And Clayfeld wonders if his sense
of this illuminated mountain's vast
impersonality can free him now
from being only who he is.
A measure of detachment from
his personal desires has broadened,
he believes, his own capacity
to care for animals and friends,
so that the very act of taking care
becomes for him its own reward.
    How fortunate, he thinks, confronting his
deep longing to transcend himself, that he
is able to conceive of selflessness—
a thought which seems to come from somewhere
far beyond his own volition or his will
and takes the form of serendipity.
The very concept of a selfless self
is like a happening without a cause
which then inspires happiness,
though Clayfeld knows that happiness
remains contingent and ephemeral.
    Yet Clayfeld chooses still to focus
on the paradox that he feels most himself
when he regards his life as if he might
have read it in a book—a life about
a lover waiting by a waterfall,

a credible alternative to what
he can remember of himself.

And, suddenly, out from the underbrush,
a startled moose emerges with its antlers
gleaming in a splotch of sun, its spittle
sparkling in its beard, smelling of urine
to attract a mate; his presence is
so overwhelming that shocked Clayfeld,
apprehending him, is shaken from his trance,
back to his solitary self.

He tastes his acid fear within his lungs
as its gigantic head, with flattened ears,
sways back and forth, about to charge
and trample him into the silent ground.
Clayfeld is flushed with the sensation of
his body's readiness to run or hide
behind a boulder or a hemlock tree
in caring for his one, his only life.

And yet in Clayfeld's overheated mind—
his mind reduced to his own dread—
he knows he is preparing to relate
his threatening encounter
with a stamping, wide-eyed moose
to a trustworthy friend—someone,
perhaps, who wonders why this story of
personal fear must mean so much to him.

Clayfeld among the Fireflies

In restless boyhood on hot summer nights,
Clayfeld would stroll among the fireflies
and capture them with just one sudden snatch;
he'd put them in a jar with holes
punched in its lid so they could breathe and flutter
in their suddenly constricted space.
　　Clayfeld was curious to see how much
illumination he was able to contain
in that diminished universe—a jar
like a transparent globe whose firmament
is made of little intermittent stars.
　　Clayfeld did not know then that fireflies blinked
their greenish-yellow lights to woo a mate
or that some females ate the males
who wished to fornicate with them.
　　Maybe desire, Clayfeld conjectures now,
despite its dietary complications,
might be Nature's compensating gift—
"a double consummation," Clayfeld quips.
Nature provides sufficient motive
to fulfill each creature's wish to replicate
itself as if into infinitude.
　　And, even more miraculous, desire,
embellished into love, appears on earth—
as Clayfeld happily acknowledges—
when given evolutionary time enough
to tinker fundamental gnawing lust
into transfiguring fidelity
as Clayfeld, too, has blundered on his way.
　　Clayfeld, as a bedazzled boy, required
no purposeful rewarding destiny
that's able to redeem a barren love;
the pleasure of accumulating light
from darting fireflies freed him from thoughts
of consequences and results,

allowing him to be absorbed
simply by snatching those elusive lights
out of the bounty of abiding air.

 When Clayfeld's glowing jar had reached
its maximum intensity, an impulse
of remorse caused him to realize he had
to let them go; his dim awareness
of mysterious distress for effort
coming to an end compelled him then
to pause in silent inwardness
and head home on the shadowed path,
curl into bed and dream—perhaps of fireflies.

 Clayfeld looks back and faintly smiles—
yes, he's amused by his compulsions and
his fantasies, and, though the information
that he's gleaned about the fireflies
illuminates the courtship rituals
of creatures everywhere, Clayfeld
remembers how their flickering attracted him.

 Briefly omnipotent, Clayfeld
could hold the glowing jar in hand—
the whirling constellation of
its pulsing lights—to be possessed,
or, like the throbbing of the summer sky,
it was a fleeting spectacle to be
delighted in with nothing further
to anticipate or to desire.

 Desire, aged Clayfeld now reminds himself,
consumes the love that it conceives—unless
love is preserved through the acceptance of
its own relinquishment, its disappearance like
the glowing fireflies released
into the dark swirl of attending air.

 Clayfeld's remembrance still contains
this surge of fireflies returning back
beyond what he was able to possess
into undifferentiated night.

Clayfeld Takes Flight

Clayfeld remembers when bald eagles
nearly went extinct some forty years ago
because vast quantities of pesticides
were spewed out over fields and farms,
which drained and leached out
into rivers, lakes, and streams
and poisoned fish eagles depended on.
The eagles didn't die right then,
but poison made the egg shells thin;
they broke before their time came due
under their parents' incubating weight
so that the chicks were prematurely hatched.
Their population dwindled, bringing them
to devastation's precipice.
Clayfeld remembers this decline occurred
the same time that the Vietnam War
was raging, and he still can picture
napalm scorching villages and forests
burned to the ground, their howling roots,
as if the devil was an alchemist
inventing formulas for massacre.
Clayfeld recalls the year precisely—
nineteen hundred sixty-two—
when Rachel Carson published *Silent Spring,*
detailing how insecticides
were ravaging the vulnerable earth,
how she was vilified by profiteers
who manufactured DDT.
And yet the ravage did abate because
of Carson's overwhelming evidence;
the stunted eagle population
started to recover from the threat
of immanent oblivion.
And now from his high mountain home,
Clayfeld spies eagles preening in their nests

or sees them plunging in the lake for fish
to feed expectant, hungry chicks.

    Eagles build nests mostly of woven twigs,
some eight feet wide, weighing a ton,
and sitting males help warm the eggs,
taking their turns at incubating them.
How gratifying, Clayfeld thinks, to learn
particularities like this—as if,
in doing so, he's able to become
most comprehensively himself:
name giver, caretaker, and guardian.
And he has actually seen and heard
a female squawk and call her mate
to offer her some respite on their egg,
which he is perfectly prepared to do.
The eagle knows one overriding truth:
it matters that the egg survives, his future
will be undivided from his past, and so
he will not hesitate to float above
the swaying evergreens, above
the human burden of uncertainty.
He knows that he must do what eagles do.

    Though Clayfeld is aware that nothing lasts,
that we destroy what we depend upon
as if to authorize our fate, he knows
we can't kill killing so that dying ends.
Beloved friends and parents vanish in
unfathomable night, never
to return except in memory;
even the sun in a mere five billion years
is fated to collapse upon itself, explode,
and burn the planet to a flaming ball,
leaving no trace of us who flourished here.

    Maybe the best that we can do—
Clayfeld's attempt at comforting himself—
is go on for the sake of going on,
unquestioning, in an eternal NOW,
without thought undermining thought,
without lethal inventiveness,

extinction's enemies, preservers of
what only can be rescued for a while.

    What are the reasons for our choosing
to endure? despondent Clayfeld asks,
a hidden silence lurking in himself.
We watch familiar images
diminish in our sight—a soaring bird,
a human face, vermillion evening light—
that can evoke in us emotions only
music has the power to express.

    The eagle is our national insignia,
another fact resilient Clayfeld knows:
and now, recovering dimmed hopefulness,
Clayfeld reminds himself this was the bird
chosen by Thomas Jefferson,
defier of oppression and lifelong
opponent of constricting tyranny.

    So Clayfeld speculates that maybe it
bodes well for our torn country at
this darkest hour, when we're a house
divided and we do not know
what we must freely choose to do
in order to be free, that the bald eagle
still survives, still circling, gliding,
mastering the wind, each one
surveying everything below,
their white heads incandescent in the sun.

Clayfeld Listens to the Aspens

    Clayfeld is thinking of his lifelong friend
while watching yellow aspen leaves
along the shaded background mountainside,
which quake and quiver in the wind
as if they are determined to maintain
their named identity in bold defiance
of the season's change to duller hues—
to bronze and then to dusty brown—
which share his mood of glum diminishing.
    And Clayfeld wonders what it is
about this momentary glow
of quaking yellow aspen leaves,
waving along white-grayish boughs,
that suddenly evokes in him a shudder
for all breathing things that hold on
as the drying aspen leaves hold on.
    He is suffused with sympathy
that summons up his absent friend
who disappeared before he had the chance
to say FAREWELL as he had wished
and make peace with the everlasting dark.
His was the laughter of necessity,
his company the sweet reward
for shared appreciation, shared regret.
    Clayfeld can hear his friend's voice in the wind;
he hears it in the quaking aspen leaves,
the undulating whisper of the lake,
the hooting of the melancholy loons,
the humming murmur of the honey bees;
his voice floats out beyond the silence
of unspoken words—the FAREWELL he
had counted on to bring some resolution
to his life that had contained their friendship
in a circular embrace. His friendship
had enabled Clayfeld to become the person

he desired to be, just by his friend's
accepting him for who he was;
he could enjoy what Clayfeld could enjoy,
as if Clayfeld's enjoyment were his own.
    Clayfeld observes the day's declining light
to see if he can find some revelation
in the quaking leaves by virtue of
their whispering their name. And yet
the leaves on pallid branches where they cling
refuse to mean more than they are;
their quaking is quite empty of
consoling thought as raucous ravens
in their silhouettes come flapping through.
    Shriveled and dry, the aspen leaves will soon
be no more than a memory of yellow swirls
turned dull to bronze, and bronze to dusty brown,
whose transformation utters its FAREWELL
with darkness darkening and merging almost
imperceptibly with the still afterglow
of lingering October evening air.

Paean for a Turtle

Mid-June, and Clayfeld
strolls along a well-worn path
about a hundred yards
from the reflecting lake. He spies a painted turtle
digging a round nest with her hind feet
just inches deep; she lays six eggs
as silently he cheers her on.
    He loses track of where he's been
while watching her produce her eggs
and cover them with loosened dirt,
trusting the earth to hatch them in
two slow months of allotted time.
Clayfeld imagines that he well could be
observing her ten million years ago—
about how long her species has survived
without the slightest need for change.
    Clayfeld is doubtful that he knows
how to account for the elation
he enjoys in witnessing this feat
of fabulous fecundity.
Sun worshippers in congregation,
drowsing on a log—that's how they regulate
their blood. Their sleek black shells return
the noon-hour blaze to the receiving sky,
which spreads its luminosity around
to simulate a halo for each turtle's head
that complements the red design
repeating underneath the up-curved rim
of their delineated shells.
    So what have you to say, enraptured
bystander, my representative,
about my turtle-praising poem,
my celebration of your celebration,
adding to your own spontaneous
response my own embellishment?

The plenitude of nature does require
the contemplation of itself to be
sufficiently fulfilled—with shining turtles
stationary in the sun, their striped necks
stretched out in embracing summer air
to feel the purpose of sustaining warmth,
as if all creatures flourish in my care.

Clayfeld Encircled

Clayfeld observes a harvest moon
ascend above the mountain's silhouette—
a perfect circle to his sight,
inviting him to contemplate a form
commencing from a starting point
that might be anywhere at all
and leads to an uncertain end.
True also, Clayfeld speculates
about our universe that hurtled out
of nothingness in a "big bang."
This vast explosion fashioned space and time
as one, and, in expanding over
three-plus billion patient years,
became the atmosphere of guilt-filled,
self-reflecting consciousness;
our words, arriving in their swoon of sounds,
now constitute, for better or for worse,
a quintessential element in which
minds mix and mingle with material.
Our fate will either culminate
in a "big crunch" if gravity—
based on the sum of cosmic mass, including
both dark matter and dark energy—
has power enough to cause expansion
to reverse, or else there's insufficient pull
to stop the universe from thinning out
and dissipating vital heat until
nothing is left but formless entropy
in which no life has power to survive,
and no last words can linger there to mourn.
Such troubled thoughts keep spinning in his head,
yet he prefers the first scenario
of a big crunch, the universe
collapsing on itself, because reversal
has a symmetry which would allow

another big bang to occur and maybe
bring new sentience to birth.
    The idea of revived intelligence
fills grieving Clayfeld with a surge of hope
that lightens his despondency:
maybe big bang explosions cycle on
for all eternity; maybe there's hope for some
improvement in the creatures that appear—
more kindness and more self-control—
to justify a process that's required
for yearning life to reinvent itself.
Hope might provide a motive to inspire
conflicted humans to endure
the suffering that we inflict
on one another through betrayal
or instinctive cruelty.
    Yet Clayfeld also hopes that he
can discipline himself not to rely
excessively on hope—and so
he circles back to thinking how
he can endure conditions as they are,
to make necessity his choice, accept
his robot hungers and his frailties.
    "Accept!" the word bursts from his lips,
and, by accepting, Clayfeld will
be able to affirm contingency,
chance sorrow, and chance happiness,
and find himself in harmony
with forces that had once seemed alien.
    He will accept by dwelling on
the pleasures of observing rounded forms—
shining, symmetrical, and smooth—
the sun, the moon, a human face, a rhyme
of apples in each outstretched hand,
since once again it's harvest time.

Clayfeld Unresolved

Composing my invented chronicle
of Clayfeld's life, his memories
of what in retrospect seem most
significant to him, I must admit
it's hard for me to tell how his
conflicted feelings differ from my own
since everything he's done I also
might have done if he instead
had been the author of my life.
　　Clayfeld remembers how his mother in
extreme old age, and blind, was able
to recall events of fifty years ago,
but nothing yesterday—Chaliapin singing
"Mephistopheles" in Gounod's *Faust:*
his presence overwhelmed the stage;
his resonating basso voice,
his cape, his stride, his dominating jaw,
left her distracted and distraught.
　　But Clayfeld's reverie of her dissolves,
and he's distracted by a woman who incites
his fantasies by glancing back at him
as they are walking on the beach,
though when he overhears her nasal voice—
too squeaky high—he's disillusioned
and accordingly depressed. He cannot find
a balm for his obsession, longing
to be rescued from his furtive thoughts
that come without his choosing them
across the intervening years.
　　And yet humiliation stemming from
the upsurge of raw appetite
is not the memory that Clayfeld
finds himself compelled to dwell on now.
He's picturing his daughter, whom he knows
cannot escape some primal discontent—

unhappiness without a cause that can
be named, identified, and thus relieved.

    Her misery is also Clayfeld's burden and
likewise my own, though not exactly mine
since his life is a variation
of my own with crucial differences,
provided I can hold invention and myself
apart, to make what is unbearable
still possible to be endured.

    Clayfeld envisions her upon a raft,
dodging the gleaming rocks in water
swirling deadly white, since danger is
the only antidote for her despair.
Wild water gathers to a hissing foam,
and now there can be no retreat,
no turning back; up to the edge she goes
and over into a black hole of
absolute oblivion beyond Clayfeld's
appalled imagining, as if she were
a swallowed star with only darkness left
for her to be remembered by.

    Clayfeld, as he's depicted here,
let me again assure my readers, is
not me, since what he suffers is
a substitute for suffering
which otherwise I'd have to master
with the aid of some chance consolation—
like a soothing wind mellifluous
among autumnal maple leaves.

    So Clayfeld goes on going on, and I—
I might as well take credit for his stamina,
his daft attempt to name what torments him,
and I'll reward him with an evening swim
across a misty mountain-circled lake
or whisk him to the opera house to hear
the rotund tenor gorgeously sing out
addio in his grief at having to depart
from the one fated woman he adores,
so sweetly sorrowful he almost swoons

with pleasure he might wish to call his own.
    Clayfeld's pale daughter looms before him
in full silhouette, right at the foaming line
before the terminating plunge
where roiling water surges out of sight—
the border called "event horizon"
by cosmologists, defining what remains
unknowable beyond Clayfeld's desire
for consolation, and beyond my own.

Clayfeld's Vampire Fantasy

I have conflicted reasons to believe
that smart-ass Clayfeld has had quite enough
of analyzing family compulsions
and fixations and hysterias:
perhaps he is some new variety
of vampire, sucking vital substance from
someone he has depended on.
"Ironic!" he proclaims out loud
to the night air, knowing he's surely got
too many ironies in his life's fire.
    Observing the pocked perigee full moon
ascend into the startled night, Clayfeld
imagines vampires everywhere
push up their coffin lids, compelled
by stark desire—or is it love?—
to consummate their needful histories.
    Wan Clayfeld weeps for them because
their fated longing can't be eased;
he weeps because his mother is
no longer there to hear him weep;
he weeps because his father can't
exhort him to control his tears
as once upon a fabled time he did.
    So Clayfeld mutters to himself in his
contorted assignation with the moon
that maybe in his reverie he is
the vampire gurgling at his mother's breast;
maybe we need, he ruminates,
each other's lives to live our own
and share each other's deaths to find
nose-thumbing gall to defiantly make
devouring death more bearable.
"Now there's an irony to feed upon!"
he chortles underneath his breath.
    Bemused by his own appetite for puns

that split their meanings from themselves,
irony-hearted Clayfeld bites
the red delicious apple in his hand
as warm juice gathers at the corners
of his lips; he lets smooth sweetness
swell and overflow and soothe the ache
that shudders in his ribs and down his thighs.
  He conjures lovers in their rocking beds,
all lavishing salacious kisses as
the brazen moon retreats, diminishes,
releasing them to dream perhaps of him,
perhaps of me, imprisoned in
snared Clayfeld's cloven ecstasy.

Clayfeld on Jury Duty

Summoned for jury duty in his youth,
iconoclastic Clayfeld claimed
that he believed humanity
had been conceived in sin as the result
of father Adam's disobedience,
assuming that the judge would then
dismiss him as impertinent,
impervious to current evidence.
    "Judge not so that ye be not judged!" taunts Clayfeld,
thinking that most famous exhortation
logically implies that one
must judge the judge that judges—therefore
contradicting the injunction not to judge.
"The mind gets tangled up in reasoning,
and thought, in contemplation of itself,
collapses in uncertainty,
and this is how," Clayfeld pontificates,
"the muddled human spectacle unfolds."
    Preparing to head home, bemused
by his own erudition and his wit,
Clayfeld quotes Hamlet's disillusioned lines
as further admonition to the judge:
"Treat every man according to his
just deserts, and who shall 'scape whipping?"
To Clayfeld's shocked astonishment,
defense rules him acceptable to serve
and seats him down among his peers.
    The case before the court is serious—
a farmer charged as his own brother's
murderer. The prosecutor lists
excruciating details of the crime:
the fallen brother's stone-smashed skull,
his teeth-stumps gaping like a grin.
The killer, his head hidden in his hands,

repeats beneath his breath, "It is not fair,"
determined to protest (how else, Clayfeld
inquires, might his words be explained?)
the accusation of his guilt as if
unfairness, not volition, were the cause
of spread blood groaning from the fertile ground.
    Clayfeld imagines that the man,
judging himself as innocent, believes
that he is the true victim of his crime,
given that nature fashioned him to be
exactly who in fact he is
and therefore doomed to be a murderer.
    The killer lifts his head, and Clayfeld sees,
as if from distant space, blue shaded markings
that surround his eyes whose agony
reverberates and spreads and seems
somehow to sanctify his presence there
because we all need somebody to blame.
    Now skip ahead some fifty years,
and once again the justice system calls,
and there again is Clayfeld trying to
cajole the judge to misjudge him
by humbly looking down in deference.
    The judge dismisses Clayfeld from the court,
and, to his vexed astonishment,
he's disappointed, feeling that the jury
is where he indeed belongs because
deliberation offers him a role
to play without protective mockery.
    The killer's features, like the moon,
revolve around dazed Clayfeld's head
amid a wilderness of wheeling stars.
Still without comprehension of his guilt
as rebel brother-murderer,
he has the stony look of permanence.
    "Am I my brother's keeper?" Clayfeld
overhears his voice blurt out as tears
leap unexpected to his cheeks,

like dew reflecting the uprisen sun,
spontaneous, impersonal,
yet somehow for himself, for everyone.

Clayfeld Throws His Hat into the Ring

Clayfeld decides to run for Congress with
a plan, he thinks, that would eliminate
crude prejudice of all varieties.
For just two generations, maybe three,
it will not be allowed to marry
somebody of your own race, religion, or
your social class, so that no basis for
discrimination will remain
after what necessarily will be
a difficult transition to an end
that justifies the stress involved
in making the unprecedented leap
to a society of total tolerance.
    To complement his radical proposal,
Clayfeld offers up his version of a policy
of "free to choose," so that a woman can
abort a child until it's twenty-one
or when he/she is able to support
himself (herself)—whichever might come first.
Clayfeld maintains his ironies
in all of his debates, believing laughter might
have some persuasive power to win
the melancholy people's votes.
    How to raise funds was Clayfeld's most
immediate concern, and so he hired
a long-lost college friend to organize
and manage his campaign. This canny friend
persuaded Clayfeld that publicity,
name recognition, is essential to
achieve political success,
and his sly strategy was to contrive
a phony exposé which would appear
in a cheap journal where he knew someone
beholden to him by a debt.
    The shocking article proclaimed

that Clayfeld was involved in smuggling
chimpanzees to labs performing tests
to see how primates would react
to drugs which caused excruciating pain.
"That's an attention-grabber," Clayfeld's friend
assured him with a pat upon his back.

As the campaign progressed, the voters
seemed to find more credible Clayfeld's
absurdities over his opponent's promises.
Clayfeld was leading in the polls
until his manager, it was revealed,
had truly been the one involved
in selling kidnapped monkeys to
the labs that were exploiting them.
His long-lost friend had used Clayfeld
as a convenient cover-up.
The very day that this fraud came to light,
Clayfeld reversed his campaign strategy
and changed his fanciful proposals to
practical legislation that would protect
the chimpanzees from torment and abuse.

Suffering, needless suffering, consumed
Clayfeld's most urgent thoughts, which now
usurped the place of laughter in his soul.
Not that Clayfeld believed humans have souls
and animals do not: "If one can grieve,
if one feels pain, that creature has a soul,"
"Clayfeld" asserted at his last debate;
"all living things share the same destiny."

Voters were not persuaded, so
Clayfeld decided that the time had come
for him to drop out of the race.
He published a confession that
his great grandfather might have been
half chimpanzee, half man—at least
according to a memoir tucked away
by his great grandmother, an immigrant
from once gold-rich, slave-trading Timbuktu.

Clayfeld's Reversal

Clayfeld goes to the hospital to have his
pacemaker checked out.
To his surprise, his heartbeat has become
more regular. His doctor can't make sense
of such unprecedented change, and orders
that more diagnostic tests be done.
The tests show would-be poet Clayfeld's heart
has gone back to a normal beat,
that his condition actually has been
restored to what it used to be
so many unrecorded years ago.
"It is as if you have regained your youth,"
Clayfeld's astonished doctor says.
"My heart beats on iambically again—
yes, iamb that iamb defines me best,"
prosodic Clayfeld quips; "no longer
can my friends call me an anapest."
"Go home and tell your wife the news,"
his flustered doctor urgently replies.
The drive home through a mountain pass,
with Mozart streaming from the radio,
leads into vistas of a gleaming lake
with a swift waterfall cascading down
a distant outcropping of rocks,
creating its own spume and mist
where afternoon reflected light
composes a twin rainbow of
surpassing clarity. Elated Clayfeld
wonders what his wife will make
of this reversal, his regaining youth.
"What if she's frightened and can't follow me
in such a turnabout?" gasps Clayfeld
out loud to himself, his spirits dwindling in
the depths of thought. What if she feels rejected

by a restoration she can't share—
as if I have abandoned her to face
declining age all by herself?
      Holding the wheel with his left hand, Clayfeld
places his right hand on his heart to see
if his grim apprehension of his wife,
stunned and recoiling from his news,
has shocked his pulsing heartbeat back
into irregularity again,
and, almost swerving off the road,
Clayfeld recalls how he first met his wife
skiing in Montreal: she was about
to plunge down the steep undulating slope,
her cheeks as red as her red hat,
flushed by a rushing surge of rousing wind.
      Yet maybe they first met in Florida
with her emerging from the sea,
her body glistening in the gold glare
of unobstructed midday sun.
What made these scenes converge within his mind?
confabulating Clayfeld asks himself;
what law of complementing opposites?
      When he arrives at home, Clayfeld discerns
something indeed is wrong. His wife looks pale
and her lips tremble as she speaks:
"I think that you've grown tired of our life,"
she says. "I think you think that you might need
something quite new, perhaps a change of heart,
to keep your so-called spirits up."
That instant, call it fate, or call it
serendipity, the flashing phone chimes out
a prerecorded Mozart melody.
A message from the hospital proclaims
that Clayfeld's tests had been misread:
his offbeat heart remains unchanged.
In a lunge, in a bump, in a bounce, in a leap,
his heart skips to its old, familiar,
anapestic beat— as when a man of grief

in a wild whirling swoon, a vertigo,
falls uncontrollably in love.
And Clayfeld feels miraculous relief.

Clayfeld Reading by the Fire

Forecasters predict "thick freezing fog,"
warning all journeyers a film of ice
upon the roads may make them slick
and dangerous. So Clayfeld thinks
he'll stay at home today, build a congenial fire
and browse a book that speculates—
as if it were a memory—about
how the Cro-Magnon newcomers
replaced the wintering Neanderthals
only some 30,000 years ago.
    And Clayfeld wonders if Cro-Magnon speech
was then advanced enough to help them
hunt together, stalk and kill
wild game that would allow them to survive.
Clayfeld remembers that he's read
Neanderthals pre-chewed their food
in caring for their aged and their sick
and thus were able to prolong their lives.
    He dozes off and journeys back
to when his grandma in her kitchen
pounded matzo balls—enough so that
she could sustain a band of rebels
in the woods against the Cossack ransackers.
Clayfeld imagines that she must have known
some secret of endurance capable
of overcoming hostile odds, raising
four children and escaping to America.
    But then grandma fades out, and Clayfeld
sees his mother at his father's funeral,
her face contorted by the wind,
although when she looks back at him
before she throws a farewell flower
in his early grave, she smiles—her cheeks
illuminated by the midday sun—

prepared to move on, she assures him,
as she must, as so must everyone.

   Then she too fades away, and in the dusk
Clayfeld, half dreaming, half awake,
discerns a shaded figure, dressed in furs,
using a crutch to limp along; perhaps
he's a remaining aged Neanderthal
receding down a tangled forest path
that disappears into a glen.

   Still at the edge of wakefulness,
Clayfeld can picture the whole family
of silent, hunched Neanderthals who sit
together in a cave around the embers
of a fire, sharing a meal picked from white bones—
the gleaming carcass of an antelope.

   And Clayfeld wonders if the starved
Neanderthals were filled with images
of summer berries in lush shrubbery,
of incantation in the flutter of
the animated forest leaves,
of leaping fish above a silver stream,
the murmuring of marsh grass in the wind,
before the strangers came, before
Clayfeld arrived to meditate, to dream,
to speak words of unspeakable regret.

Clayfeld Grieves for Annie

When we behold a wide turf-covered expanse, we should remember
that its smoothness, on which so much of its beauty depends, is mainly
due to all the inequalities having been slowly leveled by worms.
—CHARLES DARWIN

    "Reverence" expresses Clayfeld's feelings
for Charles Darwin's generosity
toward friends, consideration
for his wife's religious faith,
devotion to his many children—
Annie in particular, who died
of fever at the age of ten.
    Darwin's commitment to the truth
of how Nature designed itself,
based on examination and impartial
evidence, despite the consolation
of a Christian afterlife
that needed to be given up, has long
provided Clayfeld with a model that
he wished to honor and to emulate.
    Clayfeld believes that Darwin's theory—
evolution and descent, of how
creatures must struggle to compete
since their supplies of food are limited—
is the most powerful idea ever
conceived by humankind because
of its explanatory scope and depth:
we all remain at heart what once we've been.
Species will flourish in their time,
become extinct when circumstances change,
and vanish never to return again—
a truth not easy to accept.

Darwin thought evolution had produced
"forms beautiful and wonderful."
The "war of Nature" was a process
he described as having "grandeur,"
since increased complexity had led
in time to human consciousness,
society, and moral sentiments
like sympathy, benevolence, and trust.
    But Darwin's attitude about how
Nature operated to select the fit
kept darkening until, disburdening
himself of pent-up anguish, Darwin
wrote to Joseph Hooker, his good friend,
condemning Nature's works as "clumsy,
wasteful, blundering, and horrible";
no consolation for inevitable
conflict can be found except perhaps
through human care and tenderness,
the pleasure that we sometimes take
in bringing pleasure to someone we love
as little Annie surely did for him.
    He wrote an elegy extolling her—
"It was delightful to behold her face"—
recording her last quaint and gracious words
as "I quite thank you" when he held
her head and offered her a final drink.
    Clayfeld is dubious that evolution
can account for such unselfishness
or tell him where to look for consolation
in a world where loss, unmerited
and indiscriminate, seems absolute,
beyond repair or recompense.
    Surviving Annie's stupefying death,
Darwin continued to be burdened by
the marble weight of mournfulness,
and yet he went on working since his work
allowed for self-forgetfulness
and granted him the patience to endure.

Twenty years after Annie's death,
he wrote a book in praise of worms,
comparing worms to gardeners who
"prepare the ground for seedlings of all kinds,"
depicting worms as cultivators—first
among the farmers of the earth.
    Did Darwin find some consolation in
the laboring of worms who plowed the soil
through ages immemorial
in knowledge of renewal through decay?
Can such relief be credible? Clayfeld
is stunned to think this might be true.

Clayfeld's Inheritance

Clayfeld consults his lawyer to confirm
the wording in his will makes clear
that when he ends up in the hospital,
no special measures—lung support
or intravenous feeding—be employed
in order to prolong his life,
mere creature that he is, confronting
existential nothingness.
    If two days pass without his cracking
an old logic-twisting Jewish joke,
or if four days elapse without
a single pun escaping from his lips,
he is to be considered brain dead and,
no longer his true self, allowed
to disappear into the gaping void
with only laughing words as epitaph.
    His lawyer reprimands him, saying that
"a will is not the fit place for a joke;
death and inheritance require
solemnity so the decedent's final
wishes are precisely understood."
    "Wrong! and wrong again!" Clayfeld
cries out. "Laughter is my rightful inheritance;
my last words mustn't sound lugubrious,
so add this story—food for hungry thought
in my survivors—to my will
beside the boring legalese about
dividing up my property.
    "I drove my red Saab over slick back roads
to chauffeur my three bundled kids to school.
One day my third-grade son informed me
he was being teased by students
from farm families with pickup trucks;
they'd taunt when he arrived at school,
'Rich kid! Rich kid! Kevin is a rich kid!'

"I asked would he like me to intervene,
but, arms enfolded on his chest,
Kevin replied, 'I'll handle this myself.
Don't worry, Dad.' I told the teacher what
was going on, and next day she
reported that she'd overheard him
boast back to the other kids,
'You'd be rich too if your dad started
every day by writing poems!'
     "But then I started wondering
what might my motive really be
in writing poems: the simple pleasure
of arranging sounds in patterns with
related images; the soothing thoughts
of reaching out beyond my solitude?
     "And now I'm wondering if poems
resemble wills in that they are composed
of words they keep by giving them away—
like waterfalls that hold in place
by changing in their undiminished flow.
     "Now is the time," Clayfeld proclaims
with elegiac eloquence,
"for me to bare my best caretaking self—
as when I left a cornucopia
of apples by a bear den for the cubs
in case their mother had been shot.
     "O thought unbearable!" Clayfeld
immediately mocks himself
in his identity as guardian
of creatures capable of pain; he mocks
his need to see himself as eminent
consoler of the needy and bereft.
     And then, to satisfy his audience
and transcend mockery, Clayfeld
elects to intervene in Nature's flow
toward wordlessness with yet more tales
and willful puns punctiliously summoned
as a parting gift for everyone.

He pictures grown-up Kevin in the glow
of rosy dawn: he's holding up a bagel
that contains and circumscribes its hole
of inner emptiness—a talisman
in risible defiance of
unsmiling faces staring back at him
across the great lugubrious divide.

Clayfeld Addresses His Father

"Greetings to you, old sentimental ghost!"
Clayfeld declaims into the pulsing night.
"This birthday anniversary I'll try
to catch you up on what you've missed.
A century ago, when you were still alive,
nobody knew our universe includes
a trillion galaxies like our own Milky Way.
     "We know now that some fourteen billion years
of cooling and expanding space
provided opportunity for complex life,
against the odds, to suddenly emerge
and multiply and contemplate
the sheer good fortune of its origin,
though not so fortunate, I fear,
if some time in the distant future
energy runs out, there's no life left
at all, not here, not anywhere.
What would you make of such finality?"
     Addressing a white swirl of clouds,
Clayfeld feels compelled to speak his mind:
"I think the story of fortuitous
creation out of nothingness
provokes our questioning: can we
find satisfying purpose here
to face our cosmic destiny,
the way you faced your early death?
     "The thought of wheeling galaxies,
erupting stars, and superheated dust
condensing into planets circling on
their necessary way, producing
replicating forms here on our earth
with their astounding variants,
makes my head swirl with awe and dread—
it seems so pointless and impersonal.

"Yet somehow, Dad, it's beautiful
to contemplate: fixed universal laws,
transcendent forms, and stories
to be told for us to wonder at—
immensity so grand, with endless
improvising and inventive change.
Do you think wonder is sufficient
consolation for this pageantry
of transformation and of vanishing?

"As if revealing purposeful intent,
symmetrical designs inspire us to praise—
pinecones and snowflakes and the patterned wings
of butterflies, to take delight in
human faces whether smiling or
contortedly askew. Creation
from a void, from total emptiness,
makes speculation pause, and I forget
myself until your voice returns me
to my solitary self that can't escape
awareness of its own mortality.

"And yet I still enjoy imagining
the universe has now fulfilled a purpose
that was there inherent from the start:
to make creation conscious of itself
and multiply our pleasure being here."

Clayfeld looks upward in the night,
consumed by his own cloudy fantasy.
"I ask you, father," Clayfeld actually says,
"to offer some consoling words to ease
this burden of self-consciousness,
obsessed with future time, unlike
the untormented animals.
Is human thinking Nature's triumph
or a blunder, an incurable mistake?

"Before your voice has faded out
even beyond my wish for your return,
tell me what you believe we can—
despite what inescapably we know—

embrace and celebrate until
all matter is unfathomably cold,
all motion is unfathomably still."

Drifting and Gliding

"What's late and what's too late?" Clayfeld
conjectures to his silent self,
sitting across from his strong son
in their flat-bottom fishing boat
in late October where the river swerves
through twisted rushes and bent reeds;
it seems that they're alone on earth,
inhabiting this hidden place.

    Tall tamaracks along the mountain slope
still hold their golden needles in
declining sun, and on the river bank
stiff grasses flutter yellow, mimicking
the waterway's reflected light.

    His son allows their boat to drift
according to the stream, gliding
toward nowhere in particular
because the point of drifting is to drift,
the goal of gliding is to glide
in order to obey the river's will.

    A tree, upturned on the bank's edge,
reveals its naked roots, like intertwined
connections of a brain, dendrites
and axons tangled together
and inscrutably complex, as if about
to think a thought not known before.

    The sun descends behind a swirling cloud,
and suddenly a piercing wind sweeps in
from shaded hills as Clayfeld shudders with
a chill that quivers all along his skin.
And yet the pleasure he experienced
before the wind arose, only
a breath ago, facing his son, remains
despite his body's shivering.

    How can that be? How can his body change
but still remain the same, retaining

pleasure that has settled in his bones?
How can he feel at ease and feel distressed
at once, his brain amazingly alive,
though like the dead roots of the tumbled tree?
　　And now, below the thickened cloud,
late orange light is momentarily
contained between the bottom of the cloud
and the reflecting river's glow
so Clayfeld cannot see the source from where
the imitating light commenced.
　　His son hands Clayfeld his worn baseball cap
and says, "It's late, Dad, time to head on home
before it gets too windy and too cold."
He pulls the hissing cord that spins
the motor on and steers the boat
out of its mesmerizing drift
into the deepened purple light
now nestled in the rushes and the reeds.
　　"Goodnight!" calls Clayfeld's son as they
pass by that labyrinth of roots,
how they held on and what they knew,
and Clayfeld shuts his eyes to better hear
his son's reverberating voice
drift out in the cold wind, to hear
the water slapping at the wooden bow,
so he can apprehend and memorize
the river gliding down the darkened year.

Clayfeld's Interpretation

When Clayfeld was a teenager
he specially admired his uncle Phil,
a rabbi and a hunted anarchist—
or so the accusation went—
who had escaped from the Russian police
and emigrated to America,
where he became, so he could feed
his family, a common salesman in
a woman's fancy clothing store.
    The rabbi in him loved to quote
the Hebrew Bible's enigmatic line,
"YHWH your God will circumcise your heart,"
and Clayfeld meditated on the meaning
hidden there: something to do
with sexual restraint, or something
in our nature needing to be changed.
    Phil must have suffered childhood poverty,
but Clayfeld never asked him to explain;
he'd lost his adult teeth, and so he bought
a set of dentures, which enabled him
to flash a gleaming, unimpeded smile,
which was not able to conceal
some hint of pain that sometimes shuddered in
his lips or in the tremble of his jaw.
    In summertime, Phil and his family
would rent a country house nearby a lake
which had a sandy beachfront shared
by the gregarious community.
The ladies with their squawking kids
would gather there to gossip or complain
about their husbands, their constricted lives,
and after work a liberated Phil
would hurtle off the swaying dock
and swim far out before returning home.
    It happened that one evening Phil—

as if some thwarted force had been released—
erupted in a great volcanic sneeze;
out popped his gleaming dentures which
went rocking down into the greeny depths.

    For the remaining summer months,
the women swore that they were being
bitten on the thigh and had the purple marks
that could substantiate their claims.
Clayfeld put goggles on so he could search
the bottom ooze for Phil's rebellious
set of teeth, but all he found
were a bikini top and a barrette.

    Four intermittent wars and several
recessions have all cycled by,
whose dates help Clayfeld organize
his memories, his dim romances
and his marriages, yet he is able
to revive with stunning vividness
the story of Phil's amorous white teeth,
the ladies looking out across the lake
to apple orchards thriving there,
or shrilly titillating on the beach,
the purple bite marks on their thighs.

    And Clayfeld wonders how a memory
this ludicrous could be the agency
to circumcise his heart, seize him,
cause him to shudder top to toe,
rapt in contention with himself
as his late uncle had perhaps confessed
despite the vanities or obstacles
that destiny had scattered in his way.

    Clayfeld still sees himself down in
the muck, still searching in the depths;
rollicking laughter now evokes in him
new empathy for toothless Uncle Phil,
for all the yearning ladies on the beach,
for everyone who cherishes the hope
some transformation will enable them
to feel accepted and complete.

Clayfeld Thinks about Women

Clayfeld admires Sigmund Freud
for his abiding sympathy for humankind,
for understanding why suffering is
unavoidable since unconscious forces
do determine how we treat each other;
conflict must be stoically endured.
   Like all us guys, Clayfeld believes
Freud knew that women are a mystery;
they're more complex than reason and
analysis can make explicable;
they have their own agenda, different
from the contending energies of men.
   Married for half a century, Clayfeld
the veteran shares Freud's uncertainty
in asking, "What do women want?"
Yet he presumes to give his explanation
of Freud's most notorious enigma—
as if it were the riddle of the sphinx.
   What women want, Clayfeld proposes, is
that men should ask what women want.
That covers all the possibilities,
Clayfeld, self-satisfied, muses out loud
in silver sentences for all
his fellow males to be inspired by.
   Nature makes men and women see the world
according to divergent needs;
equality can't mean that people are the same,
philosophizes Clayfeld. Some are strong,
and some are weak; some smart, some dumb,
some nurturing, and some incapable
of trust—and this is true of women
as of men, despite the fateful fact
that women carry babies in their wombs.
   Yet men and women are the same in that
we all need food and sleep; we need to feel

we're valued and we're loved; we all
must suffer from the body's frailties;
we age, we lose our friends, we die—
and that's equality enough on which
to base our lawful rights, claims Clayfeld who
thereby has cogitated his own mood
into somber despondency.

But then the sudden wish for pot roast
pops into his head—it's almost dinnertime,
and Clayfeld calls out to his wife,
"Honey, what's on the menu for tonight?"
His wife replies, "It's pot roast—we've not had
pot roast for quite a while." This can't be more
than a coincidence, thinks Clayfeld, though
it pleases him to be anticipated
so exactly in his appetite.

Clayfeld's attention shifts again
to contemplate the fate of Oedipus,
who solved the riddle of the Sphinx
in brave behalf of humankind: what walks
on four legs in the morning, then
on two legs in the afternoon,
and then three legs at night. Aha!
It's crawling infancy, upright adulthood,
old age at last relying on a cane,
as everybody's destiny decrees.

Although he saved his city from a plague,
his universal revelation of our growth
and our decline did not suffice to help
cursed Oedipus resolve the problems
of his own tormented family,
and he remained a riddle to himself.

Then Clayfeld's thoughts segue to face
the question of Freud's questioning, of why
so adamantly Freud desired to know
what women want to know, and why,
in turn then, he desires to know why Freud
desired to know, creating a recursion,
Clayfeld realizes, that would take

his speculation whirling back
to reach unreachable infinity
with thinking about thinking about thought.
    The flavor of the pot roast lingers
on his tongue, its rich scent occupies
his nostrils' memory and makes
contentment overflow each synapse
in his roiling brain. He rises from
the dinner table, needing to repose
before the blaze in his stone fireplace,
aided by his inherited,
emblazoned silver-handled cane.

Clayfeld's Pride

For sixty years of teaching he
never had let sickness make him miss
a single class; he stayed home only when
the roads were slick with blackened ice,
and Clayfeld unabashedly took pride
in his austere reliability.
    He would admit, perhaps, his record might
have been inspired by just a touch
of plain perversity, the wish
to set a record for the record's sake,
to demonstrate his strength of will,
but mainly Clayfeld just liked talking
about books that helped him persevere
in times of stress or baffling gloom,
or deepened satisfaction in such sights
as the suffusing orange glow
of snow-topped mountain vistas or
a dragonfly's translucent wings.
    But most important to his sense of pride
was Clayfeld's imperturbable belief
in the transforming power of human will:
doubled in contemplation of itself,
beyond compulsion and desire, the mind
is able to determine who we are,
to master singular despondency.
    Yet Clayfeld knows the final test
of his philosophy will soon arrive
in how he manages his own farewell,
whether he can convey acceptance
to his children, blowing kisses to
the unresponding void, or by
reciting an old elegiac poem.
    Clayfeld enjoys the fantasy
of being circled by his wife, his children,
and his friends; he is amused by thinking

he can manage his farewell in style,
as if it might well be a comic scene
in one of his beloved operas
with interchangeable identities.

But how to view the prospects of a world
so close to blowing up, where hatred writes
mankind's grim epitaph? There is no way
Clayfeld can summon up a poem to make
bereavement such as this acceptable;
there is a limit to kind consolation
even persevering art can bring.

Lush morning light flows through the window
of the classroom, warming Clayfeld's
shoulders and his neck; his students
do not look at him, despite
his rhapsody of praise for human art;
they stare past him with faces like
reflections in a stream, and out beyond
the glowing window frame,
beyond a maple tree whose leaves
have just emerged in waves of lucid green,
to somewhere prideful Clayfeld cannot go.

Clayfeld Bedeviled

The death of Satan was a tragedy
For the imagination.
—WALLACE STEVENS

    Clayfeld slams down his newspaper
and tells his twin, "Maybe the devil does
control the world, and maybe evil is
not just synonymous with crime
but actually exists as sin.
    "Motive would have to be involved
in designating what's beyond
forgiving leniency, so punishment
can aptly be applied—damnation for
eternity as in the devil's case."
Clayfeld imagines him in a black cape
and bright red alligator shoes.
    "What guilt reduces to," Clayfeld expounds,
"is our uncertainty of how to judge
our lusts and our antipathies. How much
autonomy do humans really have without
control of DNA inheritance?"
But Satan, still erect in Clayfeld's mind,
claims that he wears red alligator shoes
to counterpoint his black mustachio.
    "We're victims of contingency,"
Clayfeld proposes to his wary twin,
"and therefore we are innocent.
We can't be counted guilty of what is
beyond volition, so we do what our
creator has determined that we do."
    Clayfeld informs his brother that he plans
to make a journey in the wilderness,
hoping to learn what might be hidden

in his heart by undergoing the temptations
Satan is most famous for, so he
can then assume responsibility
for how he treats both enemies and friends.

   "I don't employ temptations anymore,"
Satan tells disappointed Clayfeld, "since
your country honors only those
who willingly succumb to greed;
instead, I have prepared a quiz that will
expose what gets distorted in your dreams:
If god is just, how can it be explained
misfortune happens to good folks?"
But Clayfeld counters that "ever since Job,
scratching his boils with shards of pottery,
this question has remained beyond
the reach of human reasoning."

   "Wrong!" Satan cries. "You're wrong because
your premise is askew. But if your god
has no intention to be just,
the whole dilemma melts away, and I
am left to take the first creator's place.

   "I'm entertained by the vast spectacle
of suffering, and, you'll admit, that does
provide material for poetry—
tragic from your perspective, not from mine.
I dress this way because I'd like
you to believe I really don't exist.

   "So here's my second question: Why—
if I'm the sponsor of your suffering—
do I create some people truly good?"
"But that's illogical!" vexed Clayfeld
interrupts. "It violates the rule
that thought can't contradict itself."
"Quite simple," Satan, with a smile, asserts.
"I most enjoy the suffering of those
who don't deserve their pain at all.

   "The question that remains is tough,"
scowls Satan, twirling his mustachio.
"Can I—determined by myself

to be exactly who I am
with no extenuating history—
decide to change and reinvent myself?
I'd have to buy a tie-dyed T-shirt with
a slogan that can titillate your mind:
THIS IS THE BEST WORLD POSSIBLE."

Clayfeld surely is amused by this idea,
so Satan offers up a parable
for him to meditate upon:
"A skeleton wakes up one morning,
feeling ill. He calls a cardiologist
for an appointment and the doctor pokes
and scrutinizes him: SO NOW
YOU COME TO SEE ME! doctor Steinkopf says.
That's resurrection for you,"
chuckling Satan cannot help but add.

Up from a crevice in the rocks
a surge of swirling smoke erupts
before Clayfeld can summon a response
as Satan vanishes behind a tree—
the one in which a snake hangs from a branch.
His last words resonate in Clayfeld's mind:
"Disappearing is my favorite disguise;
it always wows an audience."

Clayfeld's twin brother asks, "Is this
another one of your infernal jokes?
I don't think even you know when
you're really being serious."

"I do believe it's possible for someone
to believe that legendary evil is
still possible," tongue-twisted Clayfeld says,
flaunting his tie-dyed T-shirt to his twin.

Clayfeld's "Cogito"

Seeking perspective in old age,
Clayfeld resolves to meditate
on evolutionary thoughts: how humans have
descended from their primate ancestors,
creatures like chimpanzees, about
five million years ago; how they evolved
much earlier from little mammals after
dinosaurs died out because a meteor
collided with the earth, dispersing dust
that darkened the life-giving sun.
    Humans are part of an inclusive
family of living things, rapt Clayfeld
rhapsodizes out loud to himself;
we are not set apart because we have
transcendent souls or promise of
an afterlife. Clayfeld is satisfied
that our capacity to care, even
for those who differ from ourselves,
derives from our dependency;
compassion is not handed down by some
austere commandment from above.
    Yet cruelty and greed, intelligence
to cheat and to deceive, are just
as natural as helping those in need,
and Clayfeld, thinking the unthinkable,
of evil rampant in the world,
reminds himself how violence defines
our blood-soaked history, and he
descends into the pit of gloom:
his mind cannot protect him from himself.
    "Sometimes I think, therefore sometimes I am,"
is Clayfeld's "Cogito," hoping that laughter still
might rescue him from his despair,
but baffled Clayfeld does not know
which "I" is really him—the "I" that jokes

or the "I" who's joked about.
He conjures up his rabbi friend
who suffers from arthritis of the feet
and yet gives thanks to God who is
allowing him to die from bottom up
instead of dying downward from the top.
    "Oy vey!" Talmudic Clayfeld cries, as if
there were an ancient voice inside of him.
"Too many thoughts to hold in one poor head."
Bewildered, Clayfeld thinks that evolution
blundered when it thought up thought,
though thinking sometimes makes a perfect match
with ranting age and its absurdities.

Clayfeld's Inspiration

The wisdom of embracing
the futility of wisdom offers
comfort to exhausted Clayfeld—or
perhaps (who can be sure?) it brings
more shades of darkness to uncertainty,
more trembling in the drawing of each breath.
    Wind touches everything within its reach,
as if it were the breath of some
incarnate deity residing here;
it stirs the quaking aspen leaves,
the foam fringe of uncurling waves
on the aroused, responding lake.
    Yet Clayfeld long has known the wind
has no benevolent intent, no goal
for some completion, some fulfillment
that might offer consolation or relief.
    Bent Clayfeld blows his dwindling
Yahrzeit candle out to mark the ending of
another year of gray remembering;
his breath, whether an imitation of
mild wind at morning or rough wind at night,
signifies the quintessence of
his being there inside his shaded room,
his view out to bright Venus and to Mars,
and the unknown immensity beyond.
    The aura of the winding smoke
above the wick appears as if it sought
to find a shape that Clayfeld could
identify, the ghostly shape of breath
that well might intimate the spirit of
what he aspired to do and be.
    But wisdom tells him that impermanence
alone is permanent: "hevel,"
conveying vapor or mere breath,
is the repeating word, the fixed refrain,

the ancient Preacher, Koheleth,
considered inescapable, reminding
Clayfeld of his own ephemerality—
that sorrow is the source of empathy.

    A house in mourning with soft shadows
whispering in cadences evokes
sweet reverence for those still bound within,
and intermittent rain—both sounds
in harmony like a chorale—
soothe Clayfeld's wary listening.

    Beyond his present sight, the bighorn sheep
are steady as they climb the mountain slope;
brash ravens pluck raw carrion
beside the road, then disappear
into the shade of overarching pines
as if they were wind's messengers.

    In measured silence Clayfeld stores
his silver candle holder, filigreed
with figures standing by an ancient wall,
in an oak cabinet where gently he
will dust it off again next year.
The murmured elegy he hums is almost
imperceptible upon his lips;
his body chants: "breathe out, breathe in!"
its ancient wisdom of impermanence
to soothe him in his vanishing.

Clayfeld Contends with Entropy

He knows I know that he enjoys
his disquisitions, so he also knows
it pleases me in my enabling way
to listen to him eulogize:
    "The worst is the last loss of warmth
in an expanded universe
in which the destiny of consciousness
is that there'll be no information left
to tell what once we had achieved,
no elegy that can express regret,
no lullaby, no requiem.

    "Although such cold is billions of years off,
it's not less real, less part of present thought—
like one's predictable demise—
and there's a chance we'll blast ourselves
into oblivion next week because
of murder crouching in our hearts as if
deep down we do believe our kind
can kill its way to immortality.

    "Perhaps we'll learn how to control
our immemorial desire to kill—
we're not without compassion for
the suffering of others, even strangers,
even animals; we're not without
the willingness to sacrifice for friends.

    "Maybe some momentary happiness,
some respite from tormenting thought,
remains a possibility,
some primal pleasure like the sight
of Venus in an unobstructed sky
at purple dawn. One sees oneself
as an impersonal observer, so
the idea of annihilation yet
to come recedes from certain thought
into forgetfulness, and now,

the instant in the apprehending eye,
feels like blissful eternity."
    I know Clayfeld knows such eternity
won't last for long; he can't evade
his own evasion, his denial of
his inescapably evading self,
though, strangely, he takes strutting pride
in that he's able to confront
not only absence of his finite self,
but terminal negation of all human
effort and accomplishment—our books,
our music, our sublime imaginings.
    So does it matter nothing matters in
the unsung end, or can solace-pursuing
Clayfeld soothe himself observing stellar
constellations with their fabled names
for stories of the legendary past
that seem so stationary though they are
receding at increasing speeds?
    And there is Clayfeld, gazing at a wedge
of streaking geese outlined against
the circle of a harvest moon,
embracing his forgetfulness
and listening as they pass by,
their choral cries resounding with his own.

Star-Crossed Clayfeld

for John Glendening

Clayfeld enjoys identifying stars,
seeing the constellations as old myths
described them—like the warrior Orion
or like Capricorn the fish-tailed goat.
Clayfeld imagines he's descended from
some hardy ancient seafarer
who braved the monsters of the deep
and navigated by familiar stars
in search of some exotic land, perhaps
an island filled with holy ornaments.
    Yet Clayfeld also is well read
in modern science, big bang theory,
quantum randomness, chaos complexity,
and so he knows that space and time
came into being out of nothingness
when the exploding bang occurred.
"Incredible!" astonished Clayfeld
muses to himself while wondering
if human creativity also
emerges out of nothingness, and if
all matter, everything that is,
is fated to be swallowed up
by primal nothingness again.
    Clayfeld conjectures whether the fixed laws
of mathematics—everywhere the same
throughout the universe—existed
previous to when the bang occurred,
despite the paradox that there
was absolutely nothing in the void
before conceivable space / time began.
    His meditations cause his vertigo,
though there is something quite exalting
in his dizziness—as if the human mind

deliberately was designed
for wonder and dumbfounded awe.

    Clayfeld, however, looks up at the stars
simply because he likes the show of lights—
no complicated motive there—
and it amuses him to speculate
some star-struck sailor might have been
reminded by one faint configuration of
his own protective father's goat.
Despite this pleasing possibility,
the thought of nothingness will not release
its unrelenting hold on Clayfeld's mind.

    He tries to concentrate, and once again
he fixes on the spectacle of stars:
the night sky never seemed more luminous,
a swooping meteor more radiant—as if
some meaning were about to be revealed
to free him from lifelong uncertainty.
But in that instant Clayfeld's elevated mood
collapses in despondency without
an explanation he can specify.

    Yet there is great Orion holding out
his shield against Taurus the mighty bull
about to charge with his great gleaming horns;
and there is Capricorn the goat
that suckled infant Zeus when he
was threatened by demented Chronus who,
if not prevented, would devour his son—
a goat much like the one Clayfeld had raised
when just a boy on his grandfather's farm.

Clayfeld in the Rain

For the rain it raineth every day.
—SHAKESPEARE

Clayfeld is twenty-one and hiking up
a mountainside to reach a waterfall;
a girl whom Clayfeld thinks he loves
walks with him—they are holding hands,
although he can't decide whether he should
attempt to kiss her, fearing that she might
reject his overture. They sit together
on a fallen tree, and Clayfeld stares
enraptured by the waterfall;
he watches it spin out its foam
above the darker current underneath,
forever changing, yet always the same,
constant in its inconstancy.
Clayfeld will never see this girl again.
  Now skip ahead some twenty years.
Clayfeld is leaning on a mossy bank
above a swimming hole gouged out
by a cascading stream so many
unknown years ago. A father
with his son appear and leap together
in the churning pool, but instantly
the father is sucked down, although
he manages to thrust his writhing son
above his head so Clayfeld can
seize hold of him and pull him out.
The father disappears so rapidly
that Clayfeld cannot find him when,
in vain, he dives in after him.
  The body is recovered the next day,
bolt upright in a whirlpool's vortex,

with his waving arms outstretched
as if he still were beckoning for help.
The diver says that whirlpools just like that
will form from time to time, although
they cannot be predicted; they will drag
even the strongest swimmer down.

    Clayfeld receives a note of gratitude
from the boy's grieving mother, but he never
hears from her again, nor will he write
despite his promise that he'll contact her.

    Now skip ahead another twenty years.
Clayfeld is coasting in a rowboat
in a cove among some feeding ducks,
watching them dip and shake themselves and preen,
their shimmering green heads resplendent
in the summer sun. He's tempted to
leap in the lake and swim across
to the opposing shore, so he removes
his clothes and plunges in, backstroking
to observe the cloudless sky with geese
in wedged formation testing their blurred wings
in preparation for their journey south.

    Exhausted Clayfeld tires and returns
to climb back in his boat; he starts for home,
careful not to disturb the ducks who see
no threat in him. But first he pauses,
studying his own reflection
in the lake; a ripple warps his face
as if revealing some obscure intent
contending with its opposite.
"What is this strange division in myself?
What is the water telling me?" he asks.

    To this day Clayfeld still has water dreams,
and he suspects he may have once
been rescued from the sea when he
was only two years old—the summer that
his parents had a cabin by the shore,
according to his mother's memory.
He asked her if she ever let him play

at the surf's edge with his red pail among
the swooping gulls and skipping sandpipers,
but all his mother could recall
was that his father was not well
and that her duty was to care for him.

 Again he has a swimming dream,
always with some new detail like
the churning weather or the changing light,
and yet his apprehension is the same:
he's too far out at sea—he feels
the rocking of the universal tide
and sees the waters rise up, brightening
as once they did when separated from
the firmament or when the flood
subsided in inevitable time.

 And here's another Clayfeld dream:
He's walking in a desert wilderness
as sandy wind blows, burning in his eyes;
he mingles with a milling crowd
and watches an old man, dressed all in white,
tap with his rod and magically bring forth
a surging fountain from a rock
so that the thirsty multitude survives.

 And Clayfeld ventures out into the rain,
which falls alike upon the rich and poor,
upon the young and on the old,
alike on women as on men,
on all the virtuous, all the corrupt,
on people and the same on animals,
upon the joyous and the sorrowful,
skeptics, believers, and the many who
are certain only of uncertainty
as Clayfeld certainly must now surmise:
all are alike! And so without complaint,
without dispute, without regret, Clayfeld
has no wish that it should be otherwise.

Clayfeld's Injury

"I doubt I'll ever venture forth again,"
says Clayfeld, "although that's okay,
providing I'm still able to enjoy
low echoed hootings of the hidden owls,
the snow-swept mountain vista
as reflected evening light flares orange,
darkens into purple, then to blue.
   "I'll need consoling words to help me
to forget myself, imagining the lives
of other people, real and fictional,
their satisfactions and their suffering,
what happens to them by contingency,
what sorrows they bring unawares
upon themselves and those they care about.
   "Despair won't deepen my capacity
for sympathy, and so I welcome
'melancholy' as a lilting word,
so mellow and mellifluous
it soothes the very gloom that it evokes;
and then I'll summon up 'lugubrious,'
a gasping word guffawing with
its trombone-like and crooning 'oo.'
   "And if no longer can I be defined
by how my body parts perform,
but how my words dance innuendoes
with alliterated whispers and with groans,
I'll sweetly improvise upon
the fleeting fanfare word 'farewell'
to testify that, 'ah,' I've had my romps
of bodily exuberance.
   "FAREWELL will be emblazoned in bright red
on my blue sweatshirt that I like to wear
around the house—it's optimistic
even though it does acknowledge loss
as imminent. Some rush of flourishing

is possible for a survivor who
might pause a moment to remember me.
    "So farewell ankle bones, there won't
be skipping anymore; and farewell muscles
rippling up the thigh, there's no more
climbing hills or leaping over rocks;
and farewell belly, excess and fulfillment
must remain forever unresolved;
and farewell shoulders, fingers, hands,
there's no remaining need for hugging or
the consolation of a languid touch;
farewell to eyes and ears, to naming
and remembering, to thriving just
by being here beside a frothing stream
with its attendant oriole,
dozing perhaps beneath a willow tree,
perhaps reclining by a fire."
    That's what expansive Clayfeld might well say,
enjoying the round repetitions of
his fanfare word, "farewell," with no one
at his side to overhear or judge
his motives or his truthfulness.
If I were him, I'd want to pause
without concluding whether such
recital of "farewells" might be
a potent strategy for holding on.
    Yes, I can hear Clayfeld extemporize:
"So, injured body, I'm still you
as still you're me out to the uttermost,
because a stream cascading over rocks,
a willow tree reposing in its shade,
a fire's pirouetting flames,
can only be evoked from what they are
in palpable, uncontemplated fact;
I can't dwell merely in a world of words
of 'oo's and 'ah's and warbled welcomings."
    Yet Clayfeld struts forth in his fanfare world
of mindful resonant imaginings
where injured age is just an episode—

lithe laughter in a story anyone
might find "lugubrious" enough to view
as a reverberating elegy,
pausing beneath snow-laden pines
with sunset purple shading into sunset blue.

Humming in the Air

While speculating whether music
can release one from one's isolated self
aware of its own solitude, Clayfeld,
bemused, drifts slowly in his boat,
observing turtles sunning on a log,
seeing how close he can approach before
they plunk, like one stroke on a triangle,
into the lake and disappear
in a sheer glimmer of reflected light.
    He shudders with the pleasure of
just being there, drifting with a slight breeze
cooling his cheeks and contemplating
the idea of pleasure being there,
and as he does he resonates
to thrum beats of a streaking heron's wings;
closing his eyes, he hears a humming
in the soft vibrations of the air.
    But pleasure must consume itself,
and startled Clayfeld must confront
his inmost emptiness, a blankness
looming at the outer edge of some
unfathomable dread of vanishings
and disappearances defiance can't
contain and even love can't mitigate,
and he succumbs to helplessness,
a trapped cry at the heart of quietude.
    His boat glides on, and Clayfeld hears
a western tanager's faint flute-like trill,
its iterations flickering in harmony
with its red-yellow glitterings,
and, once again, pleasure returns,
a surge of multicolored warbling hues
that pass so quickly Clayfeld wonders
if really they abided there at all;

and Clayfeld hears more humming gathered
in the lilting ripples of the lake.
      And since the turtle glowing on its log,
the tanager emerging from
a canopy of pines and tamaracks, compose
their momentary presences
in noonday radiance, and pleasure,
though not visible, is palpable,
melodious, Clayfeld considers what
his presence adds and what the universe
would lack without him pausing here
to witness its contingencies.
      Imagining the unimaginable—
his not being here—and yet beholding
a blue heron's blur diminishing
beyond his sight at the horizon's edge,
Clayfeld envisions a reposing lady
shimmering on the pebbled shore, her flute
reflecting in the noon-hour sun raised
to her lips, about to play, and playing,
and already having played, the smooth notes
flowing outward over glinting ripples
in the undulating surface of the lake.
      Attuned to voices humming in the air,
he is amused to think that she likewise
sees him reposing in her mind,
and thus Clayfeld believes her melody has freed
him from vain consolations and vain hopes
for yet another life—amazing music,
mournfully mellifluous, contrived to mean
more than mere meaning ever meant,
repeatably repeatable,
impersonal, serene, and permanent.

Clayfeld Embellishes a Willow Tree

Although old age is new to him,
Clayfeld feels that he's getting better now
at letting go, relinquishing
the dwindling wind's embrace,
the sight of redpolls at his birdfeeder,
the blur of their excited wings,
the silver of late shaking aspen leaves.
    Nothing now happening is new to him,
except that it is happening right now;
he is familiar with familiarity
and won't allow himself to wish
that anything might have turned out
differently or happier. He knows
he is what he has been, the limits
of the possible have been confirmed.
    Not far from home, he sits now by a lake
at dawn, leaning against a willow tree,
watching an orange sky illuminate
the lily pads, their yellow flowers
mimicking the blaze of looming sun.
    A bullfrog surfaces into his view,
his bulging eyes survey his universe,
including his inamorata, spawner
of some 20,000 eggs that clump
on the reflecting lake. Clayfeld extols
her contribution to posterity,
calling to her in his best booming
imitation of the blinking frog
in sentences extravagant with praise.
    And in this moment of invented
reciprocity, Clayfeld thrusts from his mind
the life that's led him where he is,
and whether anything he knows
about himself is worth recording or
best honored in its vanishing.

Clayfeld interrogates the wind to ask
if he should make an effort to remember
this effulgent, ordinary day
for what remaining time allows,
simply because it's ordinary—like
all ordinary precious life.
　　　Even his questioning about
the purpose of just gazing at
what colored light reveals—the coupled
dragonflies above the lily pad,
the painted turtle sunning on a log—
has frequently perplexed him
just as ordinary consciousness,
and Clayfeld is content it should be so
as if intentionally planned by him.
　　　Why does smooth water seem to soothe the mind,
its undulations and its little crests
repeating in their inexhaustible
variety that's almost undetectable
except for glints and gleamings of
starlike reflected radiance?
　　　Again the bullfrog bellows out
in his best baritone display as if
instructing Clayfeld how to celebrate
the lady bullfrog's fabulously
feminine fertility. She's not confused,
of course, and does not think
Clayfeld might be an eligible suitor
who has been transformed into a prince,
though Clayfeld does enjoy the fantasy.
Why not? What's wrong, he asks himself,
with such extravagant embellishment
upon the everlasting theme
of permanent impermanence?
　　　Are laughter and embellishment
evasions of the fading out
of what he'd learned to recognize:
the swallows nesting underneath the eaves,
the water ripples now diminishing

as aspen leaves go still? Or are they,
Clayfeld wonders, hesitations
and minute prolongings for whose sake
the shadow of the ordinary willow tree
is stretched out on the silent lake?

Clayfeld's Farewell Epistle to Bob Pack

Dear Bob, I want to thank you for
your interest in my memories,
my meditations, and especially
my puns and jokes, as I also partake
of what you've salvaged from the past.
We all need scrupulous attention
and response, someone to share
our follies and commiserate
with our carnal vicissitudes.
    Beneath this mellow harvest moon,
I still can picture you—a boy content
just fishing with his father from a ledge
above a foaming stream. The flailing trout
you caught is packed in gleaming ice;
the pink stripe all along its side
is smeared across black shiny dots
that seem to shine with their own light.
    I'm sure that you can picture me
with equal vividness, and though we're not
identical, there is a sense
in which I am inventing you
as much as you're inventing me.
    Like you, I've always been attracted to
the glow of objects in the landscape
of my own boyhood experience
that holds back the encroaching dark:
October gold of aspens and of tamaracks,
an orange sunset that's reflected in
a quiet lake, the tousled red crest
of a pileated woodpecker
who's hammering for insects in a tree.
    Without each other we would be no more
than an account of chance events
imperfectly recalled, imprisoned in
the body of our finite lives, longing

for love to offer a reprieve, condemned
to thinking only what is literal:
you with two wives (not both at once),
three children, lots of dogs and cats, and me
with my four melancholy wives
whose names begin with the same letter, "M"—
M as in Mortal, Mom, or Melody—
though maybe I exaggerate a bit
to wring a chuckle out of you.
   Don't try to pin my joking down
as an excuse to contemplate yourself,
a solipsist sealed off in your own
solitary world; I'm separate from you
in that I am defined by what eludes
your reasoning in order to
release yourself from clinging gloom—
the body's inescapable decline.
   It's good I still can speculate
that I have influenced your life
to modify how you regard yourself
when you reach out to think of me,
my jokes, my winged improvisations like
the sparkling variations on a flute
when you feel trapped within yourself.
   But I am more than just your alternate,
your sacrificial scapegoat offering,
despite the fact you have imagined me
as doing what you might have done
in compromising situations, driven
by some fevered lunatic desire.
   You might choose to imagine that
I can depict you watching me
the very instant I am watching you:
a boy in a canoe, his father in the stern,
paddling across a lake to get close to
a waterfall on the opposing side—
a resonating image with a rainbow
pulsing in its spray, suggesting
your emotions also overflow.

You might describe the willow tree's
evening reflection in the azure lake—
an image that conveys obscure
awareness of your being there
in temporary time and place, and yet
with place and time both permanently fixed
as if in an accessible eternity.
Such evocations are, for sure, not literal.
To hell with being literal!
And long live simulating metaphor!
    Don't get me wrong. I'm not implying that
in your imagining of me you have assumed
that I have only fictional reality.
I miss my father just as you miss yours;
I miss my children's distant lives; I miss
the company of my departed friends
with whom I could recount old pranks
and dredge up half-forgotten jokes.
    A priest, a rabbi, and a minister
arrive together at the local bar
and lean their elbows on the countertop.
The bartender approaches them and asks,
"Is this a joke?" and in my mind this scene
is animated with three hot bassoons
proclaiming, yes, it's me, Clayfeld ubiquitous,
the ever-welcome welcomer!
    I order free drinks for my customers,
the belching men and glossy women
panting in their loneliness; all clink
their beer mugs in the smoky din.
The priest says, "Blessings on you, son";
the grateful minister intones,
"The road that leads to paradise is paved with
gracious sentiments and deeds";
the rabbi doffs his shiny yarmulke,
bows to his waist, then stands erect,
his hand outstretched to rouse the multitude
of celebrating beer-drinkers
with this inscrutable epiphany:

"The God of Moses grants His grace
only to those whom He grants grace."
     And so to you, Bob, I now offer my
appreciation for providing grace
of laughter from your life's infirmities
to my own uncompleted history,
as what you see in me embellishes
the shimmer of your luminary sight—
a hopeful respite from despondent thought—
so that you're free to celebrate
a little glimpse of Clayfeld in the night.

Epilogue: Swan River in October

Shimmering crimson clouds
are now reflected on the river as
my son and I coast downstream
toward no destination
in particular. We paddle and we drift,
feeling the current in our bones,
repeating its inevitable flow.
    Ahead we see a beaver lodge
fringed with fresh branches harvested
for winter nourishment to feed
a family of six or more. A beaver
slaps the water with its thick, flat tail,
which makes a cracking sound
that echoes like a rifle shot.
    And high above, three sandhill cranes
in silhouette, with wingspans
almost eight feet long, prepare
for immanent migration south,
forming a triangle which they maintain
until they have diminished out of sight.
    A rainbow trout with its pink stripe
breaks through the surface calm to snatch a bug,
creating ripples that dissolve,
expanding into circles so symmetrical
one might imagine a designer
improvised in forms that no competitor
would pridefully presume to emulate.
    My son avoids a tree stump
lurking just beneath the mirror
of configured clouds, and I can see
a vein jump in his sunburned neck
as he swerves our wood-carved canoe
back on its course to somewhere
still to be decided as late light

begins to settle in the reeds
and in the berry-studded shrubbery.
    A doe arrives at river's edge
and adds her hoofprints to the telltale mud;
she bows her head to drink,
then suddenly lifts up as water
tumbles from her lips; her ears twitch as
she stares in our direction though,
assuringly, I whisper we
have no desire to cause her harm—
all creatures here are safe for now—
but, unpersuaded, off she goes
into the rustling underbrush.
    And now I wonder what my son
might say to me, or I to him,
beside our tended fire tonight
within a ring of gathered stones;
does something all-fulfilling
and definitive require expression
in our human words, or can
our drifting on Swan River with the twice
reflected cloud formations doubly
glimpsed in darkened colorings
inscrutably sustain us and suffice?

Epilogue: Abundance

On the east shore of Flathead Lake
in northwest Montana, weather conditions
are exactly right for growing cherries,
and for a thirty-mile stretch,
sloped orchards with receding lines
of carefully pruned trees
display white blossoms here right now
in the sun-softened mid-May breeze.
　　Abundance is the bubbling word
betokening what my dazed eyes behold,
that resonates aloud inside my head
like wing-thrums of a hummingbird,
enabling me to improvise a goddess
bathing in a stream, imbibing cherries as
thick crimson juice slips down
and stains the corners of her lips.
　　And so abundance is my theme
now that obliterating winter has
relented, thus allowing me
to apprehend this cornucopia of images—
abundance of shared laughter
with enduring friends; abundance
of framed memories: my father
placing slippers on a snowman's head
for wary, comprehending ears;
(he cut his finger when he sliced
a carrot for the snowman's nose);
my mother grooming our lame terrier;
my sister painting butterflies
reflected in a lily pond.
　　Each cherished image glows
in its containing luminosity
that cherry blossoms shed
on this mid-May occasion on
the eastern slope of Flathead Lake

There in Montana where
my wife and I have chosen well—
though blustering December snow
will blur hunched ravens huddled
on a tumbled cedar fence—
to make ourselves abundantly at home.